Looking For My Dad And I Found The Father

One Woman's Journey and Discovery in Search of Her Daddy

A Memoir

KIM CHAMBERS

Copyright © 2017 by Kim Chambers
Los Angeles, California
All rights reserved
Printed and Bound in the United States of America

Professional Publishing House
1425 W. Manchester Ave., Ste. B
Los Angeles, California 90047
323-750-3592
Email: professionalpublishinghouse@yahoo.com
www.Professionalpublishinghouse.com

Cover design: TWA Solutions.com

Cover Photography: Lacy Smith
mississippi.lacy@gmail.com

First printing January 2017
978-0-692-82001-8
10 9 8 7 6 5 4 3 2 1

No part of this book may be reproduced, stored in a retrieval system or transmitted in any form or by any means without the prior written permission of the publisher—except by a reviewer who may quote brief passages in a review to be printed in a newspaper, magazine or journal.

For inquiries contact: _____

In Loving Memory
of
Myrcia "Poppy" Chambers
June 2, 1943 to August 17, 2016

Rise Above:

Rise above, rise above all hurt and pain. You left us so soon. I wish you were here. I must rise above everything that would attempt to get in my way to accomplish all that God wants and desires for me to do. I must rise above. There are so many things to accomplish, that you and I had discussed, I have not forgotten; it is in God whom I must trust. I will rise above. Rise above anger, rise above strife. When things just do not seem right, we must rise above. I must rise above the sins of the world and live my life for Christ.

Troubles will come and go. I must not waddle in the troubles; just rise above. Mountains of obstacles may come my way, and I may not see a way around or over them. This is temporary. With God's help, I will rise above. The storms of life may come as heavy rains; I must not fear. My job is to go through the storm, and get to the other side. Don't just stand there, stay in the storm to wait it out, drown or die. In order to rise above, I must do away with excuses or pointing the finger of blame, just rise above. Only I can help myself to rise above. I must rise above no matter what; with God by my side. I will make it. I just need to rise above. You rose above, Momma, and now you are with the Lord, waiting for all of us that you have prayed for to rise above.

TABLE OF CONTENTS

Acknowledgments 7
Preface 9
Introductions 11
Chapter 1: Welcome To The Chambers Of My Life—My Story 21
Chapter 2: Was Dad Dying? Or Was He Dead Because Of Sin? 27
Chapter 3: Children Have Church, Too, So Let The
    Church Say Amen! 37
Chapter 4: My Grandfather And Uncle Were Substitute Dads 43
Chapter 5: Dad, Don't Die In The Streets. Come Home 48
Chapter 6: Choices 55
Chapter 7: My Grandmother Wanted Me To Stay Pure 60
Chapter 8: Thinking Of Marriage At Sixteen? 63
Chapter 9: I Was Wounded And Creating Baggage 69
Chapter 10: Keep Your Legs Closed 75
Chapter 11: Brother On Fire 77
Chapter 12: I Was Stuck On Stupid With The Chameleon 80
Chapter 13: Not Equipped For Marriage 92
Chapter 14: They Were Not The Only Ones Divorcing 96
Chapter 15: The Woman I Needed To Become 101
Chapter 16: Mistakes 108
Chapter 17: I Was Carrying Baggage, But The
    Baggage Got Too Heavy 113
Chapter 18: The Trickster 116
Chapter 19: Can You Come And Get Me, Father? 121
Chapter 20: No Help After The Separation ....
Chapter 21: The Forgery 127
Chapter 22: Soul Ties Have To Go Now 135
Chapter 23: God Sent Me Help! 138
Chapter 24: The Listener 143
Chapter 25: Ms. Fix-A-Problem 151

Chapter 26: Selfishness And Impatience 153
Chapter 27: I Didn't Understand The Journey 157
Chapter 28: Explaining The Baggage 162
Chapter 29: God Said, "Focus On Me, And I Will Take
   Care Of Everything Else." 178
Chapter 30: He Sent An Earthquake To Get My Attention 182
Chapter 31: There Are Two Sides In A Battle 187
Chapter 32: Sister Soldier Took Me To Church 193
Chapter 33: Leaving The Altar And Here Comes
   The Eloquent Warrior 196
Chapter 34: Sister Soldier And I At The Beach 199
Chapter 35: I Was Making Things Worse 202
Chapter 36: The Eloquent Warrior Said, "Shut Up! Consider
   The Source!" 204
Chapter 37: Tell Your Story 206
Chapter 38: How Are You And The Listener? 210
Chapter 39: How Is Your Relationship With
   The Father And Dad 214
Closing Prayer 216
His Help 217
Words I Meditate On 219
Books I Read 220
References 221

Acknowledgments

Lord, I want to thank you for my mother who has always been there to support me. She has helped me open my eyes to see the truth, even if I did not want to see it. I know she did it because she loves me. Thank you for all your prayers, Mom, and everything you have taught me throughout my life. I know you were hurting to see me go through the storms that were raging in my life at times. However, I endured to the end. God saved me and never left me. What an awesome God we serve. Whenever I felt like I was falling, the Lord stepped right on in, picked me up and carried me through. Lord, I thank you for my dad. Daddy, God told you that He loved me and that He was working on me.

Thank you, Dad, for always sending me to the Word of God for the answers I was seeking. Thank you both, Mom and Dad, for being here for me and continuously lifting me up to God. To my beautiful daughters, I am grateful to God that He gave you all a heart to love me and respect me, in spite of all my imperfections. I prayed to God a many a day to show me how to raise you up. To be able to instill the word of God in you, so that you would be able to know right from wrong and know that God is your source. Kristi Rankin, Ashley White, Gabrielle White, and Danielle White, I want to tell you that I love you and thank God for the day that He blessed me with you as my children.

What a blessing you have been to my life. I want you all to remember to never give up on the Lord because he will never give up on you. The Lord will see you through the good and bad times. I pray God's blessings and His favor over your life. Run the race that God has put you in and finish the rewards will be great. Keep striving for success in life. Aim for the stars, my sweet girls. If you fall among the clouds you are still on top. You all are predestined for greatness, so allow God to pull the greatness out of you. He has given you all individually specific gifts and talents. Ask God to stir them up. Show you your gifts and talents. May God bless you exceedingly, abundantly above all you could ever ask or imagine. May God's will prevail over your own will. You make sure you put God first in everything you do and you will be just fine.

Lord, I thank you that you are the author and finisher of my faith. I thank you that whenever I needed you, you were there. Sometimes it did not feel like you were there, or look like you were there, but I trusted in you anyway. Out of the No's is where the victory came. Everyone's journey is different. We are all designed uniquely. You said, "Every good and perfect gift is from above." Our gifts and talents are from you. I know that they were given to use, and that's all for your glory.

Thank you for getting me out of Egypt and for directing me to the land of Canaan. I thought that I was going to be in Egypt forever. It felt like you did not hear my prayers and pleas. Thank you for leading me to the land of the good and plenty. Thank you for taking me through the deserts of life and over some of the mountains that were blocking my pathway. These mountains were blocking me from your will and purpose for my life. There are no words of expression that could describe, or no songs of praise, that would ever be able to express to you, Lord, how grateful and thankful I am to you. I love you, Lord, with all my heart and soul. Lord, less of me, and more of you, Lord. It is not my will, Lord, but your *will*, to be done. I pray that you get all the glory from this day and forever more. I pray that people will hear you in this book. They will see your mercy and grace. I pray that it will make a positive impact on their lives. Lord, allow your spirit to rest on the pages of this book, in the name of Jesus, Amen.

Preface

When I began to write this book, I started reacting like Moses in the Bible. When God told Moses to go and tell Pharaoh to let His people go, Moses refused, then made up excuses. I knew that God said that there were books in me, but I had no clue how to begin. God led me to ask my niece if she could help me write a book. I did not even have a title. I just knew it had something to do with my life. My niece told me that she would help me write the book and I became excited. This was going to be a project I was looking forward to venturing into. I had it all planned out in my head. I was going to sit down with my niece, tell her my story, she was going to type it out and put it together for me. A book, just like God said. I had no faith that the abilities to write a book were already embedded in me. Moses did the same thing. He started doubting that he had the abilities to do what God was asking of him. Moses was making the Devil's job easy. The Devil comes to rob steal, kill, and destroy. Moses wanted to be obedient, but he was short stopping himself. I wanted to write a book, but my niece already knew how, so why not let my niece do it? Moses began saying that his speech was slow and wanted God to use Aaron instead. Moses was looking at the gifts, talents, or abilities of someone else. I did the same thing. I was looking at my niece's gifts and abilities. God did not call Aaron; he called Moses. God told me to write the book, not my niece. I get tickled because when God wants to get his work done, He gets it done, even if it means working with what makes us comfortable at times.

He left Aaron in the picture, but his work was going to be fulfilled. My niece has been left in the picture. She did not write the book, but she could help me with this book by explaining to me how to express myself on paper. I thank God that he blessed me with a beautiful, strong, and talented niece with a beautiful heart who helped me accomplish what God told me to do. I love you, niece, and appreciate you so very much.

I cut myself off in thought one day and remembered that, if God tells me to do something, that means He has already equipped me with everything I need to get what he needs done. The doors that need to be opened will open when he opens them. God will give me the tools needed to protect me from the enemy or enemies that come against the kingdom of God, and I am a part of his kingdom. I thank God for equipping me because I do not just want to see the promise, but I want to live in the promise. Let me tell you what took place before this happened.

In April of 2015, we had a guest speaker at our church. This anointed man of God was sent to our church on assignment to speak a word to our church. It was my pastor's anniversary celebration. The message was that we must have a spirit of celebration before the manifestation. God is about to out do what he has already done. He told us that things were changing.

He said, "Take the limits off God. Thicken your skin and get ready for the ride."

It was more to the sermon, but you just had to be there. The one thing that he said that I did not realize until a year later, while watching the DVD, the message was when he said that we needed to be focused because the enemy was going to attack. Three months later, everything started going bananas out of the blue in my life, which you will read towards the end of this book. My eyes are wide open now. Your will be done, Lord, in my life.

Introduction

I am a spiritual superhero and, while you read this book, I want you to see why I call myself a spiritual hero. A spiritual hero? Yes, a spiritual hero. I started off as a Super Spiritual Woman. I had major damages. I was broken up. I was sent to the spiritual hospital by way of a vessel sent by God.

The vessel said, "It's going to be okay, Kim. God sent me to help you, so I am going to get you to the spiritual hospital."

"Am I okay?" I asked the vessel.

The vessel did not say that I was okay. Instead, he said, "Kim, you are going to be okay?"

"How bad is the damage?" I asked the vessel, "I cannot feel anything!"

"What?"

"I cannot feel anything!" I replied in a worried and scared voice.

The vessel assured me, "Kim, everything is going to be all right. We are on our way to the spiritual hospital and the best physician there ever is on standby, waiting for your arrival. Hold on, Kim! Hold On!"

When I got to the hospital, the chief physician greeted me. "Kim, you are in my hands now and I am going to take care of you."

The hospital staff immediately prepped me for emergency surgery. Before the anesthesia took effect, I remember hearing:

> *"Things which are not seen and ear has not heard, and which have not entered the heart of man, all that god has prepared for those who love him."*
>
> —1 Corinthians 2:9 (NAS)

The chief physician took me into the operating room himself, and he went to work on me. It was going to take more than one operation to fix the brokenness that I had endured. The spiritual hospital had the right technology and the capability to take care of my brokenness. I am so glad that I was in good hands. The procedures that I had to undergo could only have been done by a chief physician. A physician that has the extensive skills, techniques, and training in all the areas that were damaged on me. The operations consisted of a spiritual heart, which gave me a new love for God. I was given spiritual legs to stand on, to make sure I walked with God and stood in his power. I was given spiritual arms to raise and give God praise. I was given spiritual hands to clap as a form of praise. I was given spiritual ears to hear what God's word said to me and to hear when God gives directions for me to follow.

Finally, I was given spiritual eyes to see as God needs me to see through the spirit of God. The chief physician had done a new thing in me. Old things were removed and they were replaced with the new. Was this necessary to do? I guess I was jacked up.

When I finally came out of the final surgery, the vessel asked, "Kim, how are you doing?"

I paused before speaking. "I feel like I am better than I was before. In fact, I feel like I am brand new."

The vessel said, "Kim, there is something that I have to tell you."

I looked at the vessel with concern. "What is it?"

"Kim, you were so broken up that the chief physician had to replace some parts of you with super spiritual parts."

"Super spiritual parts?" I asked, confused. "What is that?"

"This was a special operation that could only be done by a chief physician of his kind."

"I am confused, vessel. What are you trying to say?"

"The chief physician had to replace your heart, your legs, your arms, your hands, ears and even your eyes that you are looking at me through."

"It sounds like I have a new body. What was wrong with my old body? I have had my old body my entire life. It was not a perfect body, but it was mine."

"Calm down, Kim. You even said that you feel brand new. There were too many damages. and it was better to just replace them than to try and fix what could not be fixed."

I was just silent.

The vessel continued. "It is going to take some time for you to process all of this that has happened. You are better than you were before the surgery. You are better, stronger and quicker to receive the truth, like never. The Father had to give you a blood transfusion during the surgery at one point because you were losing blood.

"The blood that runs through you will never lose its power."

"So, you are telling me that not only do I have super spiritual parts, but I even have blood that has power?"

"Yes, that is what I am telling you. The blood not only runs through you, but you had to be washed in the blood. Why is that? Well, even though you have new spiritual parts, some of the battles you must fight here on earth, will cause some wounds to you. I cannot promise you that you will go to war and not have a scratch on you at the end of the battle. While you remain here on earth, you will run into some battles that you may find difficult to spring back into things immediately, especially when some of your closes friends and family become casualties of war.

Trying to recover, keep your head on straight and allow yourself to not give up. Staying in the race may be the challenging thing to do. The blood can wash you over again as white as snow. It will give you the ability to regenerate the areas that were wounded in battle. You will go through rehabilitation for a while, so that you can get use to the miraculous changes. If you didn't know, you should know that you are a miracle. I never looked at myself as an actual miracle.

"You must know the mere fact that you exist is a miracle. Every day that you are awakened, open your eyes, take your first breath of the day, you are given the gift of thought. The wonderful gift that the Father gave you to use the limbs that you have been given are miracles. Please learn how to appreciate the little things, but most of all appreciate the life He gave you."

"Can I read minds, too"?

The vessel laughed. "No, Kim," he said. "I know a lot has been replaced, but no mind reading on your part. I can tell you, who can read minds and that is the chief physician. That is why one of the names he is called is All knowing. The chief physician said that he will be in to meet you. He will get you through each step to make sure that your recovery is successful."

"Thank you for bringing me to Him," I said to the vessel, "and not letting me stay out there and die."

The therapy was a lot of work. I was becoming the Super spiritual woman for sure. I had newfound powers. It is awesome when you think about it. I am a walking miracle. A lot of heroes wear capes, but there was no need for a cape with me because I am covered by the blood of Jesus. For, this new blood has the power to do many things, but most importantly it protects me. I received a heart that was awesome. This heart gives me an ability to love like God wants me to love. The original heart was only half of a heart and when the heart broke, it left me with not much of anything. I would not have could survive. I needed a new heart for sure. Love is very powerful, and I needed the heart to be able to love.

My arms andhands were so powerful, as I raised my hands to praise the Father, praises would come out of my mouth. My mouth was acknowledging that God was the true God. This ability gave me new songs to sing because life had a new meaning, The Father was everything I needed him to be and more. When the praises went up to God the blessings came down on my life and began to overtake me. What a feeling it was. My life had an outpouring of blessings like a running faucet that could not be shut off.

The legs were amazing. They were strong enough to stand on God's word. I never knew how to stand on God's word before. I have heard that I should stand still and see the salvation of the Lord, but now I understand it. I stand on and up for the truth, knowing that God is with me. I need not fear because the Father is with me. Trusting and focusing on the Father is my job, The Father takes care of everything else. My ears could hear what God was saying to me—what God needed me to hear that was fruitful.

The Father trained me to listen to him because I used to have only selective hearing, which got me in a lot of trouble. These ears allow me to hear clearer. My eyes before had a distorted view when I looked at people, places and things, but now theses eyes allow me to see how God wants me to see. The chief physician truly made me whole.

The chief physician came into my room. "Hello, Kim, I am the chief physician."

"Hello, chief physician. Do you have a name that you would like me to call you instead of chief physician?"

The chief physician replied, "I have many names, Kim. You can call me King of Kings, Lord of Lords, Jehovah, Jehovah Rapha, Jehovah Jireh, Jehovah Rohe, Jehovah Nissi, Elohim, Immanuel, God, Jesus, Mighty One, Almighty, Chief Physician, of course, or just Father."

"I would like to call you Father. You have so many names, Father."

"Yes, I do. Too many to tell you. It would probably take all day. It is just that I am that I am. What about the other physicians that work here at the hospital?"

"I am the only physician here. That is why I am called the chief physician. I am the only one able to do the type of operations that you acquired from me. The other employees here already call me Father, or by one of the many other names I am known by, for I am the Father of all the living and existing. All creation was created by me."

"Father, the vessel said that you wanted me to start rehabilitation now."

"Yes, Kim, that is right. You have a lot of work to do, to be able to use your new super spiritual parts properly. It is not going to be easy, but with hard work, dedication, a willingness to run this race, you will be victorious in the end. You have to do this by faith and not by sight."

"Not by sight? What do you mean?" I was puzzled.

"You cannot always go by what you see or much less what you hear. Your flesh will want to reject your new parts, but you are going to have to be strong during those times."

"If you feel like you cannot do it by yourself, then all you have to do is call me and I will be right here. Remember, I will be here every step of the way during your rehabilitation," the Father said. "Let's get started."

The rehabilitation had many workers that helped make sure I was doing all the exercises necessary for me to achieve a full recovery. There were specific workers that were assigned to me during this process. Every time I would speak the Word of God, the workers came and carried out the Father's plans. The workers obeyed the voice of the Father. My exercises included, to learn how to pray all the time, to pray in secret, pray for those in the positions of authority, and those who mistreat me. This was important to learn. Prayer was not just for my family, but to pray the Father's will. I found out that the Father prays for me as well. I had to learn how to fast. I learned the law of sowing and reaping. Once I understood the law of sowing and reaping, I was doing my best to make sure I reaped good in my life.

I had to learn how to walk by faith. I had to learn how to listen to the Father, and walk in a way that was well pleasing to the Father. One of the toughest exercises to learn was how to praise the Father in the good times and in the bad times. It was imperative for me to do all these exercises properly because the Bible is the final authority. I was having trouble. I was making big mistakes. The feeling of uselessness was on me like a thick piece of fog.

When the vessel came to the room where the rehabilitation was taking place, a couple of months later, I told him that I felt like a failure. Trying to follow the books and to do the right thing the right way all the time, seemed impossible.

"Kim, it is okay. It is normal for the flesh to try to reject the new super spiritual parts you have."

I expressed to the vessel that I did not want to disappoint the Father after all the work He had done in me. I was apologetic to the Father. Some days were just harder than others.

The Father said, "Kim, every day is a new opportunity to do better. If you fall down, get back up. I am not giving up on you, so you hold on and don't give up on me.

"Kim, if you can trust me, believe in who I am and what I did for you, it will strengthen you to hold on when you have those hard days."

Explaining to the vessel what had been happening, the vessel said, "Kim, don't worry about it. The Father knew this was going to happen before he gave you those parts. Therefore, he said he will never leave you, nor forget what he promised you. He was going to be right with you every step of the way during your rehabilitation."

"I asked the Father to forgive me."

The vessel said, "He forgave you, didn't he?"

"Yes, how did you know? The Father is like that, when we ask him to forgive us he is faithful to do just that. Wow! What an amazing Father. Kim, soon the Father will make you a great soldier in his army."

"In his army? What do you mean by that, Vessel?"

"I, too, went through what you are going through now. Really?"

"Yes, and now I am a soldier."

"What do you do as a soldier?"

"You will rescue others and bring them to the Father, just as I brought you to the Father. But remember, Kim. You will make mistakes, but if you study the rule book, the book of strategies, the book of successful battles that were previously won by other soldiers, you will come out victorious. You also need to study the book to know who our enemy is in the world, and how to overcome him."

For three years, I worked hard at my rehabilitation with the Father along with me. I was starting to really enjoy my super spiritual parts. I think I got caught up in my abilities and lost sight of where they came from. I was focused on the vessel that brought me to the spiritual hospital. I was starting to be dependent on the Vessel to be there for me, but the Father said he was going to be with me every step of the way. I could not figure out what was going on.

The vessel started coming around less and less. You see the vessel knew that a student is not above his teacher, so he stayed out of the way so the Father could finish the work he had started in me. My world was being shaken upside down.

The vessel said, "You are losing sight of what is important. You need to go back to doing what the Father told you to do. The only thing that will last are those things that we do for the Father.

"I am not the Father," he said. "I am only a vessel and I brought you to the Father. While you were doing what, the Father wanted you to do, your life was smooth, and when you let go of the Father, it was like an earthquake was beginning to disrupt and destroy things."

"You are right," I told the vessel. "I will go back to the Father."

One day I was really depressed. I believe the Father said that he could not have me depressed so he changed me.

The Father turned me into the Super Ephesians Woman. I was out and about and I ran into a woman who needed the Father's help. Once I realized it, I raised my super spiritual arms up, started to turn around in a circle and as I was turning, I was changing into the Super Ephesians Woman. I had a new uniform that had special armor. The uniform was the color red. The red represented the blood of Jesus. I had a golden Bible that represented truth. The center of my chest had a golden R, which represented the breastplate of righteousness. The gold boots represented the gospel of peace. The gold bracelets had buttons on them that when pushed would release shields, which represents the shield of faith. The bracelets blocked the darts of the evil one. The golden helmet I wore represented the helmet of salvation. My mouth represented the sword of the spirit. Because I spoke the word of God, which is powerful, it can cut like a two-edged sword.

I was able to help someone and use the tool of prayer, after all was said and done, just as the Father taught me when I was in rehabilitation. I felt so good.

The Father said, "You are ready now. You are ready to listen now that I have your undivided attention. The Father began to talk to me more and more. He was giving me instructions, and I was making sure that I was doing all that he asked me to do and say.

The Father told me one day while I was in training that I am not from here really. He said that he sent me here to become a mighty soldier in his army until he brings me back home.

"Back home?" I asked. "Where is home?"

"Home is in heaven and you were sent here from heaven on assignment for me. When you have completed all that I need you to do here, then you will go back home."

Before I could comment on what the Father said, he spoke again. He must have seen the look of confusion on my face. He said, "No, you are not the only spiritual hero here on earth. There are many heroes here in disguise. You are one of the heroes that the Father sent from heaven and, as you go out into the world, you will meet many heroes. What do these heroes do? A much better question is, what I am supposed to be doing? All the heroes did not become heroes until they were transformed, were renewed in the mind. If you remember reading your book of instructions, your book of strategies, you should remember the part which said, "Be transformed by the renewing of your mind."

"You are not from here. I do not want you to conform to what the world does and develop the bad habits they have.

"I do not want you to become destructive. Mankind has had generation after generation of wicked people. If you do not follow the blind, you will be able to do the Father's will that is acceptable and perfect, just like the Father is. The heroes are here to save the lost in the world. The soldiers in the army of the Lord are the heroes. You cannot recognize the heroes right off the bat, sometimes because they are in disguise. They take on the appearance of mankind. They are really known by their spirits. This is the distinguishing factor. You must stay on the alert.

> "Beloved, believe not every spirit, but try the spirits, whether they are of God; because many false prophets are gone out into the world. Hereby know ye the Spirit of God. Every spirit that confesseth that Jesus Christ is come in the flesh is of God. And every spirit that confesseth not that Jesus Christ is come in the flesh is not of God: and this is that spirit of antichrist, whereof ye have heard that it should come; and even now already is it in the world. Ye are of God, little children, and have overcome them:

because greater is he that is in you, than he that is in the world. They are of the world: therefore, speak they of the world, and the world heareth them.—1John 4:1-5(KJV)

I told the Father that I remember reading that in the book. I believe I am starting to really understand everything.

The Father said, "Good because that is what I wanted to hear. It is almost time for me to release you for your divine deployment. When it is time for battle at various times, you will start to see other soldiers change into what you and they are known as, which is the heroes. Many heroes have gone out before you so you will not be alone, Some battles you will fight with other heroes, and some battles you will fight alone. Are you ready, Kim?"

"Yes, I am, Father, ready to learn all I can until it is time for me to be deployed."

This is why I call myself a super spiritual hero. This comic book introduction per se is what you will discover after reading the book is really a summary of this book. Be blessed and enjoy the chambers of my life.

Chapter 1
Welcome To The Chambers of My Life—My Story

Hello, and welcome to my world, the Chambers of my life. I thought that I would take out the time to share some of my journey, and maybe you will be able to relate. I am by no means perfect because I have a relationship with the Lord. I am a work in progress. The progress is second by second, minute by minute, hour by hour, and day by day. I have flaws and I would like to share some of my story with you.

If my people, who are called by my name, will humble themselves and pray and seek my face and turn from their wicked ways, then will I hear from heaven, and I will forgive their sin and will heal their land. —2 Chronicles 7:14(NIV)

Lord, now allow the readers spiritual eyes and ears be open, be attentive to what you would have the reader receive from reading this book.

I would like to pray for you first the reader:

Father, I ask that every individual that has been divinely drawn to this book, that it will heal and deliver them. If they, too, have experienced one or some of the events in this book, I pray that this book will somehow, some way, truly be a blessing to the reader; that this book will shed some light in the dark places in their lives. I pray that the reader reading this book will see that they are never alone. Everyone has their own cross to bear, and someone else in the world is going through similar or the same situations. Father, if the individual reading this book has not experienced these things, but knows someone else who has, who have been, or is going through these experiences, I hope he or she would share this book with that person. Let them be the vessel that you use to help someone else.

Lord, even though I have flaws and I am about to share them, let not my flaws be a stumbling block to the individual or individuals reading this book. In no way am I saying that my wrong doings were okay to do because they were not. Give the reader the understanding that I am showing my flaws to give examples of what should not be done. Give the reader the understanding that you are a forgiving God and through listening and obedience to you, their lives, too, can be changed for the better. Give the reader the understanding that their blessings will come to them. They will live in your blessings; your blessings will consume their lives through obedience and listening to you.

Lord, I thank you that even though we may fall short of your glory, you are faithful and just to forgive us of our sins. I thank you that you will give the reader a listening spirit. I pray that they learn to hear your voice and will learn to do whatever you desire for them to do and act upon it. Even if they feel they are incapable of doing what you have asked of them, they should know that you will be there with them every step of the way.

Holy Spirit, have your way. Anoint this book and allow the words on the pages to come to life. Let the words bring clarity, insight, and salvation to those who may not know you, or have a personal relationship with you. I pray that those who do not have a relationship with you will desire to after reading this book; that they will become excited about a God that can completely transform their lives. I decree and declare that lives will be changed for the better by hearing some of my story, in Jesus's Name. Your perfect will be done. I give you all the glory and praise forevermore, In Jesus Name Amen! It Is So!

EVERYBODY HAS A STORY

Everybody has a story. If you look hard enough, you will find your story within one or more of the stories in the Bible. Throughout the Bible, you can read stories and will see how the Father made a way of escape, delivered, healed, set free, saved and redeemed many. You never know who you can help by telling your story. A lot of people can be saved. You can save others from something disastrous. Your story may simply answer questions for others living in a story that they once lived in.

During the beginning of the Chambers of my life, I was asking the question, "Why me?" But, why not me? Now I see that in the Chambers of my life that, what I was going through, was not without purpose. It has allowed me to help others, and especially my children. When you have come through trials and tribulations in life, it is a relief, but you did not go through that trial for yourself. The experiences from the trials and tribulations become wisdom of what you should do and what you should not do. The wisdom to explain to someone else how you made it through. You are given an opportunity to tell people or someone, how you overcame the obstacle. Guess what? It was for somebody else. It is history being created.

The Father has told his story, which stands for history. The Holy Trinity, God, the Father, God, the Son, and God, the Holy Spirit, said, "Let us make man in our image," and they did. The first man Adam was made. Then sin, a well-known disease we know of today, was spreading like a wild fire and destroying every possible man that it could infect in one way or another. This was, and is, a deadly disease. This was terrible and God, the Father, God, the Son, and God, the Holy Spirit, said, "Let's start all over again. Things are looking bad. I decided to bring man into the world another way. This time this man is going to reconcile everything. From choosing the right woman that would give God the glory, to the blessing of her womb, to planting the Son in her womb as a seed to develop in flesh, to travel through the process to be born out of the woman is a supernatural miracle. A miracle of love, restoration, and healing for mankind. He was given the name Jesus and he, is and will forever be the cure for the disease, sin. The disease has awful side effects to it. It makes those infected by it feel good in their bodies, yet it deceives the mind. Jesus, full of grace and truth, is the final man. God, the Father, said to God, the Son, "Son, you are going to have to become a sacrifice."

"Father, is there another way?" God, the Son, asked.

"No, Son, for you must be the sacrifice to save the world," God, the Father, replied, "By this, no one will be able to come to me unless it is through you. They must take on your name, then be born again in your name."

The Son said, "They will need help."

The Father responded, "I know that is why, God, the Holy Spirit, will be left here to comfort them, lead them and guide them into all truth, when you leave. What a story! This is not how it is said in the Bible. These are my own words, but what a wonderful story. We are testimonies to someone else; that if we can make it through various trials and tribulations that come our way, so can the next person. No one is going to listen to someone that has no experience of a trial that they are going through. It will go on deaf ears. Oh, what a feeling it is, when someone understands what you are going through and can help you overcome. You may even be saying to yourself that no one has gone through what I am going through. There is nothing new under the sun, so that means someone has experienced what you are going through or worse. Have you ever heard that history repeats itself. It does in new forms. Have you ever heard someone tell somebody else not to complain, it could be worse? Do not complain because there is always someone dealing with something worse than you?

You may have even started telling your story, and after you told your story to someone, that same individual turned around and told you something that was horrible. They began to explain an event that happened to them or someone they are acquainted with and made you feel as though your trial was trivial. You may have even said, "Man, I really do not have nothing to complain about." Do we really have anything to complain about?

> *Do all things without grumbling or disputing, so that you prove yourselves to be blameless and innocent, children of God, above reproach in the midst of a crooked and perverse generation, among whom you appear as lights in the world.*
> — Philippians 2: 14-16

> *Give thanks in all circumstances, for this is the will of God in Christ Jesus for you.*
> — 1Thessalonians 5:18

I have a lot to be thankful and grateful for. I made it through many trials and tribulations, as you will read in this book. I made it because God never left me, nor has He forsaken me. He had to carry me at times, through some things and practically dragged me out of some others, but He was there. Praise God! It is so funny to think of God pulling me by my ear because I got myself in some mess, like my mother did one day when I was about six years old.

My mother said, "Kim, we are going clothes shopping and when we get in this store, you are to stay right next to me, understand?

"Yes, Mom, I understand; but I do not know what happened when I walked into the clothing store. Maybe it was something in the air. It was one of those round clothing racks with clothes on it, and for some reason, I wanted to know what was in the middle. I looked to see where my mother was and when she started looking at the clothes, I decided to crawl under the clothes to the middle of the rack.

"I did not bother the clothes. It was a smaller ring in the middle, and I decided to sit on it while my mother was shopping. I could see my mother, she did not realize I was not next to her, so I moved to another clothing rack and then it happened. My mother picked up this outfit to put up against me and realized I was not standing there next to her. She first called me in a small voice and when I did not respond she got louder. My entire being said, "Uh, oh!" I had a deep swallow because I remembered what she said. I tried to slowly come out, but she was on a level of fear that you never want your mother to get to. It was too late for me when she caught eye contact with me. She came over to where I was, grabbed my ear so hard and pulled me by my ear through the store. I was so embarrassed. Back in those days when I was little, it was a village that help raise kids per se. Those other ladies looked at me in a way that if my mother would have not gotten me, they would have got after me.

They're eyes looked as though they were piercing right through me. They had looks on their faces like, "That is what you get."

I asked for that and let me tell you. My mother never had to tell me to stay next to her ever again. I believe the Father does that to some of us at times, and I think he taught my momma that. I can only imagine. Please do not ask me why my imagination runs this way. I guess I am just hardwired like this. Let's go now and enter the Chambers of my life, shall we? All I am saying is, tell your story because everyone has a story.

Chapter 2

Was Dad Dying? Or Was He Dead Because Of Sin?

This all started when I received the most devastating news. My mother told me that my father was strung out on crack cocaine. She said, "You might as well just look at the situation as if your dad is dead." She believed that most people have a difficult time trying to recover the use of drugs. I do not believe my mother realized exactly what she was telling me at that time. She used the word *dead*.

There are many synonyms for the word dead. Words like; lost, broken, unresponsive, even fallen. Although there are plenty others; these are a few synonyms that stood out to me. The fact of the matter remained, my dad was experiencing all of these things. My dad had lost his direction for what was right, what was true. My dad was broken because it caused him to lose his self-respect, his self-esteem, his dignity, his integrity, his job, and his relationships that had great value in his life.

Dad was not conscious of the negative effects of the drug, He was unresponsive to anyone who was telling him to get his life together, or seek help for his addiction. He was unresponsive and had begun to get comfortable in his new lifestyle. He had, in fact, fallen because in his mind, life as he knew it, was over. He was deliberately disobedient to the Word of God and had completely distanced himself out of his relationship with the Lord. My mother was, in fact right. I had finally got it. She didn't mean that he was dead literally, but she meant he was dead "figuratively." Him being dead figuratively meant the man I once knew had strayed away, but it could have very well become a reality. God just had different plans for his life. My dad was, and is, a walking testimony. Dad's life testifies that even though he was living in disobedience, he still belonged to God. When God has his hands on you, no one can take you out of God's hands.

> *I give them eternal life, and they shall never perish; no one will snatch them out of my hand. My Father, who has given them to me, is greater than all; no one can snatch them out of my Father's hand. I and the Father are one."*
> —John 10:28-30, NKJV

God will never leave us or forsake us. Thank you, Jesus! We are supposed to be dead to sin, not alive to it.

> *"In the same way, count yourselves dead to sin but alive to God in Christ Jesus. Therefore, do not let sin reign in your mortal body so that you obey its evil desires. Do not offer any part of yourself to sin as an instrument of wickedness, but rather offer yourselves to God as those who have been brought from death to life; and offer every part of yourself to him as an instrument of righteousness."*
> —Romans 6:11-13, NIV

Yes, we sin and fall short of His glory. We are in no way perfect, and we make mistakes and will continue to make mistakes because we are each a work-in-progress. My mother explained to me that my Dad had lost everything.

"Everything, *everything*!" I said to myself. Confused, I asked my mother, "What do you mean?" I was so confused. How could he have lost everything?

"Kim, he lost his apartment, job, cars…everything!" Mother said expressively.

After my parents divorced, my little brother went to live with my dad, and I went to live with my mother, so quite naturally, I was going to inquire about my little brother. I wanted to know where they were going to live. Would he be on the streets with Dad or staying with another family member? I did not know what life was going to look like now that things had taken such a drastic turn. I was hurt, confused, and worried.

My mother, at the time, was not sure about any of the details on my brother and father's whereabouts, but she was going to find out. I heard everything she was saying, but the mere fact that my mother was telling me that my Dad was on the streets had gotten to me. This was any child's worst nightmare.

With tears streaming down my face, I said, *"This cannot be happening..."* I looked at my mother, so upset and hurt.

"No!!!" I cried, "That is my dad and he is not *dead!*" I could not believe my mother was saying this to me. It was disturbing.

"Well, I am trying to tell you what is going on with *your* father. I do not want you to be in the dark, or get angry with me later, asking me why I did not tell you. I know you love your dad. It hurts me, too, but there is nothing I can do about it," Mother said genuinely.

IT'S A PART OF LIFE

Writing this, and reading it, I guess one could say, "Well, that is nothing to worry about. Nothing to get too stressed out over...get too upset over, or even to lose sleep. This type of situation has happened to a lot of people."

This, many times, is a response from people who it has not happened to. It is very easy to make accusations, judge others and give opinions when we are not affected by a circumstance.

I used to tell my children to never say what they would never do because "never" can turn into eventually "will." You must be careful of the words you choose; they can turn around and bite you in the rear end. I realize that it could even be said that there are several girls who have been subjected to this same situation. Girls who have Dads strung out on crack cocaine. I remember hearing people say over the years that in every family there is one strung out on drugs of some sort within various households. This is nothing new. That's life...*they say*. You are right; it is life. In understanding that there are lessons to be learned in life and when we go through these lessons, the question is, are we learning from them? Or are we just existing?

In not learning the lesson, it just continues the cycle, and one re-lives it until they get it or get over it. Unfortunately, some never get it or get over it because they feel the problem is someone else's, never them. They belong to that special group called, "pointing the finger." One day I was watching a video on the internet of these two dogs. The owner had these two dogs sitting in front of her, and she asked the dogs, who did it? Do you know one of the dogs picked up its paw and pointed at the other dog. (Laughing out loud). The people in the group must have brought their pets with them. Too funny!

How many of us are victims from the pointing-the=finger group? Peter, one of God's disciples, was a victim of the group called, pointing the finger.

What do you mean, Kim? When the twelve disciples were at the Lord's supper, they were all wondering who was going to betray Jesus. Once Jesus said to Judas, "What you do, do quickly."(NAS) Jesus tells the disciples where he is going they cannot come. Peter begins to ask why can't he follow right now. Jesus tells him he will later. Peter says that he would lay his life down for Jesus, (Peter was ride or die for Jesus). Jesus asks Peter would he lay down his life for Him. The question was followed up with a statement of facts that Peter would deny Him three times before a rooster would crow. We may believe that Peter meant well. Peter loved Jesus.

When people from the group pointed the finger at Peter, to point Him out as being associated with Jesus, he denied Jesus. When the finger is pointed in our direction, will we do what is right, or will we do what is wrong? There is a blessing in learning the lesson. Every problem has a solution. For every poison, there is an antidote. If you are a person who presently does not know how to solve the problems you are having, it does not mean there is no solution for you. I was hurting. Could things get any worse? When you think that things cannot get any worse, think again. You may say not true and I disagree.

Things can get worse, but it will never be more than you can bear as a child of God. Remember our lives are living testimonies for others, not for ourselves. When we make it through, we can minister to others and tell them how you made it through. We never should look at a situation from one view--your view—because someone else can see something totally different than you that makes sense, or is a much clearer view than yours. However, there is an amazing and wonderful savior that will guide you out of the hurts and pains if you will allow him to. It may be a part of life, but knowing I am not going through life all alone, is a blessing.

DAD GAVE ME A TREASURE

I remember my Dad coming to see me. He was explaining to me what happened to him and that what I heard from my mother was true. He was on drugs and homeless, but he was going to be all right, not to worry. This was an impossible reality in my mind. I guess in the process of my dad selling some of his belongings and trying to figure out who could hold some important things of his, he entrusted me with his Scofield Reference Bible. Of all things, he could have possibly given me to take care of for him, he gave me a *Bible*.

I tell you, I held on to that Bible as if I was given a treasure. My dad wanted me to keep it for him. When I look back and think about this Bible given to me, my dad gave me a very valuable treasure. I just did not know it at that time. This treasure held the keys on how to live the life God intended for me to live. I just had no clue as to how to go about using it. This treasure is a treasure that one wears in their hearts. This treasure is the kind of treasure that has many treasures within it. Some people call the Bible, *Basic Instructions Before Leaving Earth*. It could stand for *Building Individuals By Learning Every day*. What do you mean by this, Kim? We as believers are to study to show ourselves approved, according to 2 Timothy 2:15 (KJV); 2Timothy 3:16, 17 (KJV); Psalm 119:11 (KJV); Deuteronomy 11:19-23, My point is that it is a treasure.

that their hearts may be encouraged, having been knit

> *together in love, and attaining to all the wealth that comes from the full assurance of understanding, resulting in a true knowledge of God's mystery, that is, Christ Himself, in whom are hidden all the treasures of wisdom and knowledge.*
> **—Colossians 2:2,3 (NAS)**

> *and if you look for it as for silver and search for it as for hidden treasure, then you will understand the fear of the Lord and find the knowledge of God.*
> **—Proverbs 2:4,5 (NIV)**

The only way that you can get to the treasure is by opening the Bible up and begin reading. The more you learn from what you have read, the more you change. Notice, I did not say the more you read, the more you change. You will become more like the Father. You will develop a relationship with the Father. Applying what you learn from the treasure will change you. Your day-to-day living will cause you to see life brand new. You will never be the same after opening the treasure. Some changes you will see immediately and some changes will happen over periods of time. It has changed me and I like who I have become and excited that each day I awake is a new opportunity to learn something about the Father.

DAD'S BACKGROUND

Allow me to give you a little background on my Dad. This is not about his life, but descriptions of the titles, roles, and positions he had in his life before and up to the drug addiction, which lead him to the streets. My dad was in the United States Army, served active duty for four years before being released with an honorable discharge. After the Army, he was married and he divorced. Years later, he married my mother, and my mother talked him into going back to school to get his GED. My dad went to a junior college. There he took the required courses and obtained his GED. My dad was saved and in the church, studied Hebrew, was well versed in scripture and became a Deacon in the church.

He worked as a janitor for two year before becoming a traffic control officer for the city of Los Angeles. He did so well in Traffic Control that they told him to apply to become a Los Angeles Police Officer. He did just that and remained a police officer for 12 years. After serving on the force, he became a leadsman for a heating and air conditioning company and later started his own business, JC AC heating and air conditioning. My oldest sister's father had a plumbing business, so he and my dad partnered up together to help each other's business grow. This meant that if my dad had an air conditioning job and the customer needed plumbing work done my dad would recommend my sister's dad and vice versa. Business was great and a guy that worked with my dad introduced him to crack cocaine. Unfortunately, everything has a root and the door that opened that was the fact that my Dad was smoking marijuana for recreation, not for medicinal purposes. He not only smoked on his own, but with a worker who was into getting high on a whole other level at the time.

This was a problem and my dad lost everything behind an addiction. Dad was on a journey to rock bottom, whether he realized or not. Was he not going to be able to come back up top until he knew what it felt like to walk, to sleep, and to live on the streets? Was this solely about an addiction? Or was it something else? This was my dad and I did not understand. My dad went from business man, to the streets, to prison.

WHY WAS DAD GOING TO PRISON?

My uncle, my dad, and my ex-husband had my dad over on this one day. My uncle, his brother, and I were asking him when he was going to stop what he was doing and come off the streets. I will never forget my ex-husband stopping the conversation. He looked at my dad and asked him in a nutshell was he ready to stop smoking crack. He went on to say if my dad said yes, he wanted to continue smoking, then we would just leave him alone and we would not bother him about it again. My uncle and I agreed. My dad said that he did not want to stop right then. It hurt us, but we let him go. That evening everything changed for my dad. The thought of my Dad being in the streets on crack cocaine was devastating. Well, it is a miracle that I did not lose my mind when I found out that he was going to prison. Your dad went to prison? Yes, he did. I remember the first phone call I got that night that he was in jail, saying he was going to have to go to court. The police were going to prosecute him.

I asked my Dad what happened. He said they were going to let him go, but when he took off his cap and a crumb size piece of a rock (crack cocaine) fell out of his hat, the officer decided to send it to be tested. The results came back that it was crack cocaine. This was totally mind blowing. A man that once was a policeman, himself, was now going to be a prisoner in a state correctional institute. I asked my dad was he going to be in protective custody because of his former status and he told me no. I was so upset, he told me that he was going to be placed in general population because he did not want to be alone, he rather be around people. - Around people! Around people! Are you kidding me? I felt like my dad must had lost his mind. When does the need to be around people override your safety?

I was thinking to myself, does he want to die? Does he have a death wish? I cried, cried, cried, and prayed. It is very sad when people cannot be comfortable in their own skin. They cannot be alone, a person that needs to be needed by anyone. Needing to be needed by anyone can bring the wrong type of people around you. You need them and they use you. This is not good. It was nothing I could do about this situation. I was worrying so much, I began swelling all over. My feet would swell so I had to wear shoes two sizes bigger than my actual foot size. Yes, I was worrying even though that is a sin. I must be truthful. I was stressed out so much, I got sick. I began breaking out in hives. I was not even eating and I was gaining weight. Who wants to get fat? I was already over-weight. Most people lose weight when they don't eat, but what happened to me? I was blowing up like a Goodyear blimp, (Laughing out loud).

It was not that I did not exercise, because I did. I remember when I was taking an aqua aerobics class and I was getting dressed in the locker room. As I passed the mirror on my way to the pool, I noticed my thighs in the mirror. Man! The cottage cheese is real. As a figure of speech, it had left the refrigerator section of the supermarket and jumped in my thighs.

When the class started, the instructor worked us out so much that I thought he was confused because I had never been to an aqua aerobics class that worked you out like a trainer at a gym. We were not on the ground. We were in the water and I was sweating. This was not a little sweat; I was sweating profusely. I know what it was, really. This was a pool with a Jacuzzi in it—right? No, it was just a pool. I was not the only one in the class that felt this way. There was a lady that was saying that it was hot in the pool.

I began to say, "No, it is not the pool; it is us. You know when you go to the store and you buy a chicken to cook at home?"

She said, "Yes."" She was looking like what does the chicken have to do with the sweating."

"Okay, you know when you get the chicken in the sink to rinse it off, and cut the fat away from the meat?"

She said, "Yes."

"That chicken is us." She chuckled.

"You see these arms and legs that have all these dimples in them? That represents the fat against our meat."

"You know when you bake chicken and the fat melts and becomes the grease at the bottom of the pan?"

"Yes," she says, laughing.

I continued. "So when we work out we are like that baked chicken, (she is laughing hysterically). The harder we work out, the more we sweat. That is the fat melting off, so let's just workout until it melts off."

That lady looked at me and laughed. She had never heard an analogy like that before. I had not either, (Laughing out loud).

We both laughed.

The stress was too much. I had reached to the point where I was just fasting for weeks, praying and asking God to protect and hide my father's identity, which God did. To God be the glory forever more.

God is our refuge; He is our fortress, He is our present help when we are in need. Daddy had a two-year stretch and the entire time that he was incarcerated, I was praying for his protection. My only form of communication with my dad was letters and an occasional collect call from a correctional institution. The calls were expensive so he would write me.

Chapter 3

Children Have Church, Too! So Let The Church Say Amen!

This is not about my dad's life story, but my dad was a part of my journey. I am what you would consider a Daddy's girl. Like I said earlier, my parents were divorced. They had gotten married before I was born, stayed married for twelve years and got a divorce. When I was a baby. My parents were in the church and I was dedicated to God by the pastor of the church. My grandmother used to tell me that God's hand is on my life. She could see it when I was a baby. She said when I started talking and I would be in church I would mimic what the pastor would say. I cannot remember accurately, but I believe after age three, my parents stopped going to church often.

The devil comes to rob, steal, kill, and destroy. He does not like marriage according to the way God designed marriage to be. When I was five years old, I wanted to be saved. This experience that I am going to explain to you is not the experience that most people would expect. For instance, when you are at a church and during the altar call, you walk to the altar and tell the pastor, "I want to be saved."

This was totally different. Allow me to share. One Sunday, my grandparents and cousins had just left church. The church that they attended had church service in the main sanctuary and the children had church in a different building on the same premises. It was called Children's Church. The Children's Church back then was set up just like it was in the main sanctuary.

They had their own choir, ushers, and an appointed minister that was anointed to teach the children the Word of God. On this particular

Sunday, my cousins asked me if I was saved. Allow me to try to give you a visual of three five-year-olds and a two-year-old having church service at home. One five-year-old female evangelist, one five-year-old male preacher, one five-year old female being lead to Christ, and one two-year-old female as a member of the church. The evangelist holding her tambourine and Bible in her hands asked me was I saved.

"Saved? ...What do you mean saved?" I asked confused.

The preacher holding his Bible in his hand says in his preaching voice, "Yes, saved, filled with the Holy Ghost, been water baptized?"

While the preacher is preaching, the evangelist and the member of the church are saying, "Yeah, Yeah, Amen!" This was a mutual way for the congregation to agree with what the preacher was saying with few words, which is common among members of a Baptist or Holiness church.

"No, I am not saved," I said sadly.

The preacher says in his preaching voice, "That means, if you are not saved, you are going to hell." He spoke in a very convincing way.

The evangelist and the member of the church, chimed in, "Yeah!"

"What is hell?" I asked.

The evangelist responded, "That was where the devil lives. You don't want to go there, do you?"

The preacher lifted his Bible and opened it to the scriptures. "All those who are not saved will go to hell and burn in the lake of fire in the end with the devil."

The evangelist started to shake her tambourine, saying, "Hallelujah! Hallelujah!"

The tears started rolling down my face. I said, "I don't want to go to hell. What can I do to be saved?"

I remember my cousins telling me that all I had to do was to confess with my mouth and believe with my heart that Jesus died on the cross for my sins. Jesus rose again. To confess that I did not believe in Satan, I believed in Jesus, and I now belong to Jesus. I said it all and they said I was saved. Can you picture three five year olds and a two-year-old praising the Lord, and the preacher saying, "Devil you lost another one?"

Out of the mouths of babes and sucklings hast thou ordained strength because of thine enemies, that thou mightiest still the enemy and the avenger.
—**Psalm 8:2, KJV**

"Do you hear what these children are saying?" they asked him. "Yes," replied Jesus, "have you never read, 'From the lips of children and infants you, Lord, have called forth your praise?'"
—**Matthew 21:16, NIV**

"Now you have to be filled with the Holy Ghost," the evangelist said. Lost, I asked, "How do you do that?"

"Yeah! You have to tarry, even if it takes all night," she said.

"Tarry? " They were confusing me left and right.

The evangelist sent the member of the church to the bathroom to get some tissue, which I was going to soon find out what that was going to be used for. The preacher and the evangelist told me to get on my knees, raise my hands up above my head and say thank you Jesus or halleluiah until the Holy Spirit took over my tongue.

"Take over my tongue?" I asked.

They said, "Yes, you will begin to speak another language to God."

The tissue was for me drooling during this process because they said I could not stop. They didn't even want me to swallow. It was too funny.

Nothing happened so the evangelist said, "Just keep doing it whenever you get the chance. Don't give up."

And because the Evangelist said, "Do not give up; God hears you."

I did not give up. Many adults do not realize how smart children are. The mind is a very powerful tool that stores all types of information and puts the information in a memory bank. I believe the person or persons who came up with the idea of computers understood this about mankind and found a way for a machine to do the same.

Mankind has a problem with limitations. Mankind limits others based on their individual limitations and when the limitations are challenged they do a study. Well, the machine is not accurate, nor is man. Machines get viruses, so does man and they both have to get a cure or else they will be destroyed. Well, computers are holding more memory and are able to do more, of course, because of man, think about it.

The preacher then said," Now you need to be water baptized."

They suggested me getting baptized at their church, so I ran to the front of the house to my mother. This is where the adults were in the kitchen. Back in those days the adults would always send all of the kids to a room to go and play or outside to play, which kept children out of grown folks' conversations.

My mother was standing by the kitchen table, talking. I started tapping my mother, saying, "Excuse me. Mom."

I tugged at her shirt, "Excuse me, Mom." I exclaimed, trying to get her attention.

"Hold on, Kim," she said impatiently.

It seemed like she was not going to respond fast enough, so I began to say it again, "Excuse me, Mom…excuse me, Mom."

"What is it, Kim?" she said, irritated.

"Can I get baptized?" I asked curiously.

"What, Kim?"

"Can I get baptized?The evangelist and the preacher said I can be baptized at their church," I exclaimed. "I don't want to burn in hell, Momma." I pouted.

"Kim, what are you talking about?" my mom asked, frustrated.

"I need to be baptized, Mom, so that I do not go to hell and burn in the lake of fire."

My mother said, "Kim, I don't want just any preacher laying their hands on you."

"But, Mom," I said, starting to cry, "I do not want to burn in hell." Tears filled my eyes.

My mother said, "No, Kim…we will talk about this later and mommy will explain things to you."

Disappointed, I said, "Okay," and ran back to the preacher and the evangelist, crying.

They consoled me. They were just as anxious and determined as I was to get me saved. We decided to run some water in the bathtub, so the evangelist took off her dress, she was in her underwear and slip. The preacher took off his suit. He was in his t-shirt and shorts, and I was in my t-shirt and underwear. We were in all white for baptism so they could baptize me right there in the house.

We got in the bathtub and unfortunately, while they were baptizing me, we got caught and got in trouble. I guess we got too quiet and the adults went to look for us. I can only imagine what was going through their minds back then. Being that I am now a parent, they probably thought we could have drowned.

> *Children, obey your parents in the Lord for this is right.*
> **—Ephesians 6:1, NIV**

> *Children obey your parent in everything for this pleases the Lord.*
> **—Colossians 3:20, NIV**

It was always in the back of my head that I did not want to burn in hell, and that I needed to be baptized. During the summer, I use to go over to my aunt and uncle's house to visit. This was my Dad's brother. I was about 11 or 12 years old, and my aunt and uncle went to church all day on Sundays. Sunday school, morning worship, and evening worship. One Sunday morning during morning worship, the preacher did an alter call and I walked up to the altar and told them that I wanted to be baptized. I got baptized.

> *As they travelled along the road, they came to some water and the eunuch said, "Look, here is water. What can stand in the way of my being baptized?"*
> **— Acts 8:36 (NIV)**

I did not tell my mother because I thought she would tell me I couldn't do it. I did not like the feeling, that I was keeping this a secret, but I was happy because I was not going to hell. I was saved. She found out of course from my uncle because that was news to celebrate. This moment in my life should have been a big celebration shared with my parents, especially my dad. This was a life-changing event and his absence, in this case, was not due to him being on the streets, but my parents being divorced. Believe it or not, I believe that was the beginning of the journey, of me looking for my dad. My mother was a single parent. My mother did what she felt was best for me as her child, and I should have told my mother. It shows you how, when certain events happen in your life, that you can carry them through your life and it can affect decisions that you make. I did not know that eight years later, I was going to rededicate my life to the Lord and be baptized again. Kim, you got baptized again?

Yes, I felt that my life was spiraling downhill fast. I did not want to go to hell for my lifestyle and I wanted to clean up my act. July, 17, 1989, I was baptized in the name of the Father, and the Son, and of the Holy Spirit. I had no idea what was going on in my life, concerning baptism. I thought I was fine spiritually and saved. Before I got married, I started attending a church with my ex-husband. I was told that I had not been baptized into our Lord Jesus Christ, so before I got married to my ex-husband, I had to be re-baptized, otherwise, we would be unequally yoked. So, on July 5, 1992, a year before I got married, I was baptized. Sometimes the decisions some people make are not based on logic. Some decisions you make can be that you were manipulated into them. Decisions should not be based on our emotions. Our decisions should be based on what is the right thing to do.

If we do not understand, we need to be educated, so we know why we are making a specific decision. There are those who feel like they need to be re-baptized because they have lost their way, but all you have to do is repent, which means to turn away from those things that are sinful. Ask God to forgive you, then re-dedicate your life to Christ and forgive yourself.

Chapter 4

My Grandfather And Uncle Were Substitute Dads

My grandfather and my uncle, whom I love so dearly and appreciate, were the only Dad figures I had in my life during the times my dad was in the streets. Unfortunately, my dad was not functioning in the capacity as a Dad, completely. My uncle, which is my Dad's brother, had a family of his own. He was so unselfish that he held a space in his heart and made time out of his life to be a father figure for me. My aunt and uncle were what I call my summer parents. I loved my grandfather. He was a great man, hardworking, and an excellent provider for his family. He was a father to my aunts, my mother, and to his grandchildren, he even raised three of his grandchildren, and one of his great-grandchildren.

He had an unconditional love for his family. He never had biological children of his own and yet you would have never known. What an amazing man. He was the only grandfather I ever had a relationship with. I can't thank my grandfather and uncle enough for stepping up to the plate as men and Dad figures in the participation of raising me.

When it was time for me to get married, I had a difficult decision to make. I had both my grandfather and uncle there for me. I had a very difficult decision to make in deciding who was going to walk me down the aisle. I chose my uncle because he was my Dad's brother to give me away. He was the closest to my Dad because he was his brother. These men are, and forever, will be heroes to me. Thank God that the Father put these two men in my life to be a covering for me in the absence of my dad. It truly takes a village to raise a child. Some villages could be friends of family and neighbors.

I could have very well become rebellious to them because they were not my dad, but I was not. I do not know many men, much less women that take out the time to make a difference in a child's life. I am not saying they do not exist, because they do. I had two men step up for me. My mother was raising me, but wherever help was needed concerning me. they stepped up to the plate when and where they could. I find myself doing the very same thing now. Anytime I can make a difference in a child's life, a younger woman, a young man, I try to do it. These children and young people can be from the neighborhood, your family, a job, and even at your church, they are all over if you open your spiritual eyes, ears, and heart, you will be drawn to them.

To be truthful, I wanted my dad as my dad. Looking back at the time, I was a Daddy's girl, yes, but I felt like a parent when I began to worry or become concerned about where my father was, and if he was safe. Unfortunately, my dad got comfortable being in the streets. I remember him telling me that he did not have to worry about bills and rent. I told him he did not have a roof over his head that he could call his own. He could not take a shower, bath, or enjoy the other basic amenities that come with having your own. On the streets, you own nothing and cannot keep anything. It is here today, gone tomorrow; that alone should have set off bells in his head, but it did not.

I went and found my Dad in a hobo camp. When God said that he would take care of our needs that was what he was doing. In the hobo camp, they had turned a barrel into a barbeque pit, which was there stove. they had a bucket they put dish soap in and water to wash their dishes. My dad had made a home under the trailer of a big rig truck. He had a bed, a dresser, and a night stand. It was unbelievable. The home lasted until heavy rains came and soaked him out, or washed him out. In the hobo camp, there were trailers and dumpsters full of clothes bundled mostly, I guess to be taken to a salvation army or to be shipped somewhere. Everybody in that hobo camp did not have to worry about clothes. The daily provision my dad needed was met, even though he was living on the streets.

My dad did not beg anybody for anything. He worked and supported his habit. He did not stand in front of business establishments or at the gas stations begging people for money and food. Even though he is a Veteran, he did not walk around or stand on a corner, especially knowing that the Veteran Administration takes care of their own, playing the sympathy game. He did not come around family begging for help or breaking in our homes to steal something from us to sell. Now, before I got married, I had to go to the hobo camp to find my dad. It was there that I asked my Dad would he give me away in marriage. I told him that I would rent the tuxedo, get him the shoes, and pay to get him a haircut, my dad said yes, but he never did. He did not call or get in touch with me. Years later, I found out that he was embarrassed and did not want to embarrass me. He was concerned about what others thought, instead of what it meant to me as his daughter, but I forgave him. I was and still am…a Daddy's girl. I have given you a little background.

I DISCOVERED THE KNEE-PRAYING MINISTRY

These things led me to my knees. I discovered how to fall to my knees quite often because I missed my dad. A desire to have my dad in my life turned into a prayer life. I find it so awesome that when I look back over my life now, I can see how God always had his hands on my life.

> *As for me, far be it from me that I should sin against the Lord by failing to pray for you. And I will teach you the way that is good and right.*
> —1 Samuel 12:23, (NIV)

I truly had begun a life of fasting and praying without ceasing. Remembering the prayers clearly. Lord, keep my dad safe. Lord, please get my dad off the streets. Lord, get my dad off drugs. Prayer was all I had, and yet it was all I needed. At the time, I did not know prayer was the key. Every time I was able to see my dad, I wasted no time. It was a constant need to remind my Dad that God loved him and was here for him. I believed that he would remember everything that God had ever said in His Word. I was believing so much that God could fix this situation, that I did not have time to have doubt in my mind. I never gave up. Giving up on my dad was not an option. It was the actual driving force inside of me.

You may ask the question, did you think that he would never come off of the streets? The answer to that question was I did not have it in me to think any other way. I loved my dad and had high hopes for him getting off the streets.

One day, I was watching a pastor on television. He was preaching, and while I was listening to the message, this phrase caught my attention; He said, "Perfect love cast out all

fear." He paused before continuing. "The only job I have is to believe that God can." Amazing, my only job is to believe that God can. It seems easy to do, but it is not. The love I had for my dad casted out all fear. It casted out the fear of where I had to go to find him and what I may had encountered along the way. I never had a concern of what could have happened to me. Instead of fear, I had courage and believed God could change my dad's life. God can do anything, everything, and yet He will never fail.

Belief means faith, confidence, and trust in someone or something, and that is what I had. Strong belief is what I had. I believed that my Dad was strong enough to turn this situation around because of his love for me as his daughter. That he would somehow realize that family was more important than the addiction he had. I had to learn this with any addiction, it does not have to be a drug addiction. There are all forms of addictions. I think of addictions as spirits and these are spirits that do not respect anyone, especially the individual it is oppressing. I look back on the times I was out searching for my Dad. I asked myself the question, Why didn't my dad just tell me to go home when I was searching for him in the streets.

Why couldn't he have said, "Kim, go home. This is not the place for you," or, "I am a grown man, Kim, and I am not your responsibility, so go home." Maybe even, "I am your dad and I love you! But Dad has a problem that you cannot help me with Kim, just pray for Daddy and go home."

I can go on and on with questions, but my dad had a problem and no matter what, I loved him. It could have been my persistence, him knowing that I was not going to listen to him, if he told me to go home. I say this now, but these questions were not in my mind at the time. I believe that we all ask ourselves questions after the fact in different situations that have come up in our lives. My only thoughts were of my dad getting off the streets and off the drugs. I did not want to lose my dad to the drugs nor to the streets.

Chapter 5

Dad, Don't Die In The Streets. Come Home.

The addiction had taken over so much that I do not believe he was sure of what he wanted himself. Dad had been living on the streets for more than ten years. Continuing to feed your addiction makes it stronger. Addiction spirits will cause you to lie, steal, kill, and destroy with no remorse. Addiction spirits have no boundaries for their path of destruction. You cannot tell an addicted person anything. When it comes to their addiction, they know it all, they think. Fools despise wisdom, and I believe addicted people fall in this category.

No addiction has overtaken you that is not common to man. God is faithful, and he will not let you be tempted beyond your ability, but with the temptation he will also provide the way of escape, that you may be able to endure it.

—1Corinthians 10:13 (ESV)

Be sober minded, be watchful. Your adversary the devil prowls around like a roaring lion, seeking someone to devour.

—1Peter 5:8 (ESV)

Do not be deceived; "Bad company ruins good morals."

—1Corinthians 15:33 (ESV)

I never put a time limit on my Dad getting his life together, either. Just awaiting the day that my Dad would say, "Enough is enough! No more street for me…God has a better plan for me!"

When you desire something so bad that you will not take no as an answer, was where I was mentally. Were there times of total desperation? Yes. I was trying to figure out what would be the triggering factor. What word, or words, could I possibly say that would be the turning point in his life. The bad part about this is that desperation is an area that the devil uses against you, as was explained to me. Desperation can attract you to things you normally would not be attracted to, make you do things you would normally not do.

When I saw my dad, I would say, "Dad, you know the Word of God. You were a deacon in the church at one time."

Dad would say, "Yes, Kim I was."

I would then reply, "Well, don't you know God loves you?" Just trying to find the right words to say that would wake up my dad. I was not one who studied the Word of God at the time, but scriptures would come out of my mouth like a river flowing.

> *It reminds me of the scriptures that said, "And the Lord said unto him, who hath made man's mouth? Or who maketh the dumb and the deaf? Or the seeing, or the blind? Have not I the Lord? Now, therefore, go, and I will be with thy mouth, and teach thee what thou shalt say.*
> **—Exodus 4:11-12, (KJV)**

In my desire to see him off the streets and in prayer, God always gave me the right words to say that were encouraging or uplifting to him. He would always agree, but he had freedom of choice and, looking back on those times, my dad had made the choice to be in the streets. His mouth did not say it, but his actions did.

> "Dad," I would say," The Lord said that he would never leave you nor forsake you. The just shall live by faith. Trust the Lord with all your heart and lean not to your own understanding."

Truth is, I was desperate. With my dad living in the streets, how could I rest? It was difficult not knowing what was going on with my Dad while he was on the streets. If I had not heard from him in a while, I would be on a search campaign. It was not like I could call him or see him at any given time. When I wanted to see him, I had to find him.

The streets were not a place for a young girl, a young woman, a wife, or a mother of children. Yes, this had been going on for years. During all that time of Dad being on the streets, I was getting older and a lot of different life changing events were occurring in my life. While all of this was going on, I would never stop looking for Dad. Through the years, my Dad stayed in motels, hotels, under bridges, abandoned homes in South Los Angeles, on the streets, even in a hobo camp, and none of these places were safe for me to be. When I look back, God was protecting me the entire time.

> *No weapon formed against me shall prosper.*
> **—Isaiah 54:17, (NIV)**

God hid me and had a Guardian Angel assigned to me, protecting me from harm and danger. Completely hidden in places that were not safe for me to be.

> *For in the time of trouble he shall hide me; he shall set me up upon a rock.*
> **— Psalm 27:5, (KJV)**

> *For he shall give his angels charge over thee in all thy ways.*
> **— Psalm 91:11, (KJV)**

My mother became very frustrated with the fact that I would never stop searching for him. She could not stop me from looking for my dad.

She would ask me, "Why, Kim? Why must you insist on looking for your dad?" She would be so upset with me.

> *When you're down on your luck, even your family avoids you-- yes, even your best friends wish you get lost. If they see you coming, they look the other way out of sight out of mind.*
> —Proverbs 19:7 (MSG)

Trying to explain something I did not know myself was difficult to do, so I would tell her, "Mom, I cannot explain in words why. It is like something inside me, pulling at me. It would not let me let my dad go, or give up on him."

> *But if I say, "I will not mention his word or speak anymore in his name," his word is in my heart like a fire, a fire shut up in my bones. I am weary of holding it in; indeed, I cannot.*
> —**Jeremiah 20:9, (NIV)**

This fight to get my dad off of the streets was truly like a fire shut up in my bones.

> *For thou wilt not leave my soul to hell, neither wilt thou suffer thine Holy One to see corruption. Thou wilt show me the path of life; in thy presence is fullness of joy at thy right hand there are pleasures forever more.*
> —**Psalm 16:10-11, (KJV)**

Some things in life will not always have an explanation. Life's mysteries are things that are difficult or impossible to understand. Mysteries are hidden. Mysteries are also revealed by the Holy Spirit.

But it was to us that God revealed these things by his Spirit. For his Spirit searches out everything and shows us God's deep secrets. God is orchestrating his plans and purposes for our lives, we are directed on paths blindly, but God! God has the light turned on at the end of the path. God is light and all things that need to be revealed, will be revealed in God's time.

—**1 Corinthians 2:10, (NLT)**

Because you will not abandon me to the realm of the dead, nor will you let your faithful one see decay.

— **Psalm 16:10, (NIV)**

What do you think? If a man owns a hundred sheep and one of them wanders away, will he not leave the ninety-nine on the hills and go to look for the one that wandered off? And if he finds it, truly I tell you, he is happier about that one sheep than the ninety-nine that did not wander off. In the same way your Father in heaven is not willing that any of these little ones should perish.

—**Matthew 18:12-14, (NIV)**

And we said to my Lord the boy cannot leave his father, if he leaves him, his father will die.

—**Genesis 44:22, (NIV)**

One thing I did know, was that my dad could die on the streets, but I was not giving up. He was going to know that he was loved, no matter how far in the gutter he fell. I fought so hard through prayer and fasting, for him not to die. When I started writing this book, I decided to look up the meaning of the word leave. Leave means to depart, to go away from, withdraw from, disappear from, or to absent oneself from. With dad on the streets, not in a stable home, he departed. Dad's addiction to drugs drew him away from people he knew and loved, he was withdrawn. When Dad lived in various places, he disappeared and was absent from being the upstanding citizen and Godly man he once was, and I once knew.

Then Moses summoned Joshua. He said to him with all Israel watching, "Be strong. Take courage. You will enter the land with this people, this land that God promised theirancestors that he'd give them. You will make them the proud possessors of it. God is striding ahead of you. He's right there with you. He won't let you down. He won't leave you. Don't be intimidated. Don't worry.

—**Deuteronomy 31:7-8, (MSG)**

No one will be able to stand against you as long as you live. For I will be with you as Iwas with Moses. I will not fail you or abandon you.

—**Joshua 1:5 (NLT)**

For the Lord loves justice, and he will never abandon the godly. He will keep them safe forever, but the children of the wicked will die.

—**Psalm 37:28 (NLT)**

God will never walk away from his people, never desert his precious people.

—**Psalm 94:14 (MSG)**

Everything in my spirit would not let me leave my Dad alone. God is true to His word. He will never leave us or forsake us. Looking back, I believe God was using me as His vessel to help my Dad, and remind him that no matter what has happened; God was still here for him. I would remind my Dad that Jesus died for all his sins on Calvary.

The debt was paid for his sins. No matter how bad things looked, even though he may have reached rock bottom, God was still with him. Man will not be with you always when you need them, but God will. We can come to Him with our whole self. All Dad had to do was call on the Lord and he would deliver, heal, and set him free from the bondage. We can be our own worst enemy and the devil knows it. We actually give the devil too much credit for our own self-will. What I am trying to say is that we have the ability to choose. We make choices and there are consequences for every choice we make, whether it is good or bad. When we enter places in this world without our armor of God, we are defenseless...*alone*. God told us how to put on the whole armor of God to protect us as we go into the world.

> And that about wraps it up. God is strong and he wants you strong. So take everything the master has set out for you, well-made weapons of the best materials and put them to use so you will be able to stand up to everything the Devil throws your way. This is no complete physical at a doctor's office that we'll walk away from and forget about in a couple of hours. This is for keeps, a life-or-death fight to the finish against the Devil and all his angels. Be prepared. You're up against far more than you can handle on your own. Take all the help you can get, every weapon God has issued, so that when it's all over but the shouting, you'll still be on your feet. Truth, righteousness, peace, faith, and salvation are more than words. Learn how to apply them. You'll need them throughout your life. God's Word is an indispensable weapon. In the same way, prayer is essential in this ongoing warfare. Pray hard and long. Pray for your brothers and sisters. Keep your eyes open. Keep each other's spirits up so that no one falls behind or drops out.
>
> —**Ephesians 6: 10-18, (MSG)**

Chapter 6
Choices

One afternoon, I was having a conversation with one of my daughters about choices. Daughter: "Mom, why is it so easy for people to judge one another ?" Me: "Well, it is simple. Think outside of the box for a minute. (Pausing in conversation). Me: Why do you think it is easy for us to judge one another? (Waiting for her to gather her thoughts, I continue speaking.) Me: When Adam and Eve ate from the tree in the garden, what kind of tree was it? Daughter: (My daughter looked at me, as if she was in great thought and said). "The tree of knowledge." Me: "Correct," I said, *(Excited that she remembered).* I continued the conversation saying that.

Me: In the Bible, Genesis 3:5 The serpent said that the day that Eve would eat of the tree, that she would know good and evil. She chose to eat of the tree and give fruit of the tree to her husband. Genesis 2:9 tells us of two special trees that were planted in the garden and one of them, which Adam and Eve ate from, was the tree of knowledge of good and evil.

I began to explain that we have the knowledge of good and evil. We are able to judge what is good and what is evil. I had her attention, so I said, let's go a step further. I explained that we are made in the image of the Holy Trinity, God, the Father, The Son, and the Holy Spirit. God is a judge over all judges and we also have cultural differences. People are raised differently around the world, according to their customs and traditions. Our right in America can be wrong in another country. Wrong and right varies from household to household, as well. If it were not for the Tower of Babel situation, mankind trying to build a tower up into the heavens, we probably would not have had so many differences of rights and wrongs.

We had to be adventurous, and creative, right? Mankind would have all been one people and one language all on one accord.

We have the choice to choose the right or wrong thing to do. It is wrong when the law is broken, but again laws vary around the world. The variations in laws and customs makes rights and wrongs different. Do you see why it is understandable that we as individuals are prone to be more judgmental. We know mankind has a choice to choose, right or wrong. We know something is wrong to do, yet we still want to do it. Allow me to give an example. We put ourselves on a diet and find ourselves in a doughnut shop. We know that we can not have a doughnut on this diet, yet we look at the doughnut through the glass and the doughnut is looking back at us. It will be bad, we know, if we eat the doughnut. You are smelling the delicious aroma from the doughnut, telling yourself, I *cannot have the doughnut because it will be all bad*, but you can-not get over how good the doughnut looks.

You and the doughnut begin to have a conversation:

You: Hey, doughnut! You know you are really looking good! You're looking all nice with that icing on you. Just looking luscious .

Doughnut: Yeah, I see you, too!

You: You know I cannot have you right? I am on this diet.

Doughnut: Why don't you just go ahead and take a bite?

You: Yeah, I want to bite you. I want to eat you all up. Doughnut you know that you are no good for me.

The reality is clear. You know that you can not indulge. Yielding to the temptation is unwise. You know it is going to cost you for indulging, yet you are seriously considering doing it anyway. The temptation is real.

You: Well, it will not hurt to take a little bite. What's a little bite between doughnut and human? If loving you is wrong, I don't want to be right.

It is real bad when we know what is good for us and choose not to accept it. A good example would be broccoli. Broccoli is good for us to eat, yet we do not want to eat it, unless it has something that is not good for you on it. You are at home and you go to the refrigerator, hungry. You see broccoli. Broccoli is all green and bushy. Nobody wants broccoli, then the conversation begins.

Broccoli: Hey, I am good for you!

You: No! I do not like the way you look. You are all bushy.

Broccoli: Well, looks are deceiving.

You: Well, this is a big deception!; You are bushy, green, and you look tough!; You look rough around the edges.

Broccoli: But, if you eat me, I will be nutritious for your body. I'll keep you healthy and strong.

You: I know, but doughnuts look and smell better. Doughnuts are smooth and creamy, and you are rough!

Broccoli: But, didn't you say looks are deceiving?

You: No, you said looks are deceiving! But I agreed with you. When I look at you, I do not want you, I know I need you, but I just do not want you. I know you're right for me, but I don't want you.

I had fun with this analogy, but when I began to think about the doughnut and the broccoli, I saw something amazing. The doughnut is round with a hole in the middle. The circle is infinite, it never straightens out. It is a hole in the middle, symbolizing something is missing. This reminds me of sin. Once we step into it, it will take us in a vicious circle, creating a hole in us--emptiness. The broccoli is a stalk, like a tree with branches. One branch connects to another branch, ever growing. This reminds me of salvation. You are constantly growing in the Lord, and the Lord leads and directs your path in life. As you grow, the Lord brings people into your life to lead you to salvation.

CRYING OUT

When we are defenseless, we become totally vulnerable, helpless, and powerless. We become susceptible to the attacks of the enemy. I needed my dad in my life. I needed my dad to protect me, teach me, pray for me, and have a father-daughter relationship. This was very important for me to have my dad, not only in my life, but as a part of it. The imprint my dad stamped in my mind as a little girl was that he loved me. I was special, important, beautiful, smart.

I could do anything I wanted to do in life. The devil has been the author of deception since he deceived Eve in the Garden of Eden. He starts talking to us and we talk back to him when our spiritual man is malnourished, or we do not have the proper covering.

> *Now the serpent was more subtle than any beast of the field which the Lord God had made, and he said unto the woman, Yea, hath God said, 'Ye shall not eat of every tree of the garden?' And the woman said unto the serpent, 'We may eat of the fruit of the trees of the garden.'*
> —**Genesis 3:1-2, (KJV)**

Then we go into justify of our sins. We lie to ourselves, others, and the devil agrees. He is the father of lies.

> *But God did say, "You must not eat fruit from the tree that is in the middle of the garden, and you must not touch it, or you will die."*
> *"You will not certainly die, the serpent said to the woman.*
> —**Genesis 3:3-4, (NIV)**

It may sound crazy, but it is reality. We stay in the sin and believe it is good. It feels good to our flesh. It looks good to our fleshly vision. It temporarily satisfies our fleshly hunger, and the longer we stay in the sin, the flesh gets stronger. Sin takes control and we start trying to get others involved in our sins. We automatically become drawn to others already involved in the same sins.

In **Genesis 3:6-7**, The woman saw the fruit was good for food and what did she do? She got her husband involved. I thank God that He is all powerful. That He loves us enough to help us out of our sins. What I have come to learn about sin is that it hurts us and those close to us. Sin torments our minds until we start looking for a way out. Crying for a way of escape, peace of mind, and so forth. You will either say, somebody please help me, or Lord, help me!

We began crying out because of what once felt good, looked good, sounded good, smelled good to the flesh is now destroying our mind, body, and soul. The aftermath of sin has made us feel embarrassed, ashamed, disgusted, uncertain, insecure, feeling of no self-worth, loss of direction, and fearful. We begin to hide and point the finger of our demise towards others because it is easier to blame others, than to blame ourselves. Who wants to admit that they are wrong? Genesis 3:8-12 is a perfect example of that. It has to be someone else's fault things are not going right in our life. This game today, as many will call it, the Blame Game! Thank you, Lord, that you had a plan on how to save us. Thank you, Lord that you loved us!

> *"This is how much God loved the world. He gave his Son, his one and only Son. And this is why; so that no one need be destroyed; by believing in him, anyone can have a whole and lasting life. God didn't go to all the trouble of sending his Son merely to point an accusing finger, telling the world how bad it was. He came to help, to put the world right again. Anyone who trusts in him is acquitted; anyone who refuses to trust him has long since been under the death sentence without knowing it. And why? Because of that person's failure to believe in the one-of-a-kind Son of God when introduced to him.*
> —**John 3:16-18 (MSG)**

Chapter 7

My Grandfather Wanted Me To Stay Pure

When I was about thirteen years old, my grandmother would preach not having sex until I got married. I think she was afraid my cousins and I were going to experiment. I was so tired of being asked if I was having sex, and if I let a boy lie down on top of me. Or I was constantly being told I would get pregnant if I did allow a boy to lie down on top of me. I was not into boys like that, at the time, but I guess she needed to scare the idea out before it settled in. Staying a virgin until marriage was drilled into my head over and over, and the importance of being a virgin.

I found out recently that my grandmother had some tragedies that occurred in her life. I believe out of her fears, she was drilling her granddaughters, even though she was telling us the right thing to do. It is unfortunate that some of us say or do things out of fear. The things that you fear can overtake you. What I mean by that is that a person puts so much energy in their fears, that they bring it to life in a sense. In the end, my grandmother's fears could not stop what you will soon read that happened to me.

Virginity is important. If it were not important than Jesus would not have been born of a virgin. Isaiah 7:14, and Matthew 1:18, 21-23 are scriptures that speak of a virgin woman that will conceive a child, a son and his name would be called, Immanuel, God with us. A virgin has not been touched so her body is pure. A pure and Holy, Righteous God came into this world through a pure vessel, miraculously. Have you ever wondered why a person who has given up their virginity finds it hard to let go of the very first person that they gave up their virginity to in a relationship, if the relationship ends?

Some women feel like they have lost everything when their relationship ends. I believe it is a result of woman giving the one true treasure that she has, which is all of herself, that is everything. The woman has attached herself, bound herself to the man, and is in covenant with him. These women are creating blood covenants (blood ties), as an agreement as being one with the man. There are lot of women in covenant with abusive men and find it hard to get out of the relationship. The people in relationships who do not break up normally stay together until death do they part. If the couple gets married first, they tend to stay together or work harder than the average couple to make the relationship work. The feeling of having a lot at stake, a lot to lose, weighs heavy on the mind. In my grandmother's own way, she probably was trying to prevent that from happening with her granddaughters.

I am sure she just wanted her granddaughters to do as God had commanded in the Bible. Even though we were her granddaughters, I am sure she wanted to make sure that she instilled serving God and doing what He says in His word, to have a blessed life. The conversation was annoying, but her intentions were good. It stuck with me in my heart and mind like a lamp needs a bulb to have light, it stuck with me. I respected my grandmother, she was not perfect, but she was an example of a godly woman and wife. I learned so much from my grandmother, not just staying virgins until marriage, but living our lives for the Lord, honoring and reverencing the Lord. She taught us to put God first above all else and I thank God for her, so much so that, I wanted to honor what my grandmother said. I wanted to be obedient. Did I confuse you? Well, I hope not. All of these things led up to the adventure, which is known as Life.

Life does not always go the way we plan for our lives to go. My grandmother was setting a godly foundation, but when we try to do what God says, the attacks come on our lives. The attacks come in the areas that mean a lot to us, examples, our mother, father, sister brother, husband, wife or even children. Staying pure is not just about virginity. Staying pure in your marriage, not allowing outside influences or people to come in and contaminate what is pure and holy unto God, remembering the vowels you made to one another. Staying pure to your relationship with Christ, leaving the old behind and continue working on staying fresh and new in Christ. Staying pure by living your life wholesome, clean, day by day, by working at keeping polluted elements and people away from you that would lead you to destruction. We must work at staying pure from impure thoughts.

I understand more now than back then, but I am grateful for my grandmother. It is said that it takes a village to raise a child, but God was using my grandmother as a vessel to instill the Word of God in a village, which was her eight grandchildren.

> *At the same time came the disciples unto Jesus, saying, Who is the greatest in the kingdom of heaven? And Jesus called a little child unto him, and set him in the midst of them, And said, Verily I say unto you, Except ye be converted, and become as little children, ye shall not enter into the kingdom of heaven. Whosoever therefore shall humble himself as a little child, the same is greatest in the kingdom of heaven. And whoso shall receive one such little child in my name receiveth me.*
>
> —Matthew 18:1-5 KJV

> *For the promise is unto you, and to your children, and to all that are afar off, [even] as many as the Lord our God shall call.*
>
> —Acts 2:39 KJV

> *And all thy children shall be taught of the Lord; and great shall be the peace of thy children.*
>
> —Isaiah 54:13 KJV

Chapter 8

Thinking Of Marriage At Sixteen?

When I got to the stage in my life of being interested in dating, which was the age 16, my mind was going in circles all the time, trying to figure out which direction I should go. My mind was a loud symphony, so many thoughts were playing in my head at once, but I had no conductor. I was always trying to find my dad in every relationship. Every relationship that I got into, I was praying that it would be the man I was going to marry. Crazy. It was difficult because I was always the one all in and assumed that if I treated the man I was seeing like a king, then he would surely want to commit himself to me and be faithful to me. What is a king?

According to the law of Moses, God has to choose the King of Israel. A king has two roles. One role besides doing his king responsibilities is to search out and to reveal things. The other is to teach things and impart wisdom to his people.

> *It is the glory of God to conceal a thing; but the honor of kings is to search out a matter. The heaven for height, and the earth for depth, and the heart of kings is unsearchable. Take away the wicked from before the king, and his throne shall be established in righteousness.*
>
> —Proverbs 25:2,3,5 (KJV)

The men that I was dealing with were God's children, but they had not decided to live the life of a Godly man. I was too young to expect that from them and they were too young to commit. I was in the wrong head space. I had too much idle time, which is the devil's workshop. I was searching for a type of love that I did not know I needed or how to get it. It was escalating out of control. This is how I know I was searching for right thing the wrong way.

I was entering relationships, looking from a Fairytale view. I was looking for stability, commitment, and loyalty in every relationship I was involved in. Every man has these qualities deep down inside, right? All they had to do was tap into that part of themselves, right? I was about to find out that everyone does not think like, nor see like I do. This was going to be a shocking revelation because I did not want a temporary relationship for me. I expected to date then get married. Why were you trying to get married? Were your hormones racing and you just wanted to have sex? No, I wanted to just be in one relationship, with one man for the rest of my life. My hormones were not an issue. In every relationship, I was hoping the next relationship would be perfect and the final relationship for me. When I look back on that time in my life, what comes to mind is the story of the Samaritan woman at Jacob's well. In John Chapter Four, verses seven through nineteen. Jesus asks this woman for a drink of water.

The woman wanted to know how he could ask her for a drink of water, being that Jews did not have any dealings with Samaritans. God eventually says to this Samaritan woman to go and get her husband. She replies that she does not have a husband. Jesus agrees, but tells her that she has had five husbands. He was all up in her business, but isn't that the way it is supposed to be. The Father is all knowing and has a love for the broken and downtrodden. People may want to throw you away like garbage, say you are not good enough, or acceptable to them or for them, but the Father loves everything about you. There is nothing new under the sun.

I had married these men that I was involved with, not in the ceremonial type of way, but in a covenant way.

> *God honored the Master's body by raising it from the grave. He'll treat yours with the same resurrection power. Until that time, remember that your bodies are created with the*

same dignity as the master's body. You wouldn't take the Master's body off to a whorehouse, would you? I should hope not. There's more to sex than the mere skin on skin. Sex is as much spiritual mystery as physical fact. As it is written in scripture, "The two shall become one." Since we want to become spiritually one with the master, we must not pursue the kind of sex that avoids commitment and intimacy, leaving us more lonely than ever-the kind of sex that can never become one. There is a sense in which sexual sins are different from all others. In sexual sin we violate the sacredness of our own bodies, these bodies that were made for God-given and God-modeled love, or "becoming one" with another. Or didn't you realize that your body is a sacred place, the place of the Holy Spirit? Don't you see that you can't live however you please, squandering what God paid such high price for? The physical part of you is not some piece of property belonging to the spiritual part of you. God owns the whole works. So let people see God in and through your body.

—1 Corinthians 6:14-20(MSG).

Thank you, Lord, for delivering me out of all that mess that I put myself into. Did you hear me say at age 16 and up, I was looking to be in a permanent relationship? Of course, you did. I do not know any 16-year-old boys that are even thinking about a marriage. I am trying to get you to understand my mental state of mind during this stage of my life. These thoughts should not have been on my mind at 16. My thoughts should have been; hanging out with friends, finishing high school, going to college, seeing the world and living. I was an emotional wreck. Over the years, I was seeking a mate to marry, which was out of order. The Father did not instruct me to go out and find a mate. He wanted me to seek his kingdom and all of His righteousness.

> *The man who finds a wife finds a treasure, and he receives favor from the Lord.*
>
> —Proverbs 18:22(NLT)

I look at some of the relationships that I was involved in and when I read the story of Jacob, Leah, and Rachel, I met myself in the story. You met yourself in the story? I may have not met myself but, I saw myself in different scenarios. Remember in the chapter, *Everybody Has a Story*? I said, if you read the Bible, you can find yourself in the Bible? I saw myself in at least seven scenarios, in the story. This is what happened to me, let me share.

Scenario 1. Jacob saw Rachel as beautiful. (Rachel) I was liked for my outer appearance and the man (Jacob) never was interested in getting to know who I was inside. This Jacob was interested in me looking good on his arms and sleeping with me. I was a prize possession, his trophy, shoulder piece to brag and boast about. It was not important whether I had intelligence or not.

Scenario 2. Jacob was married to Leah but wanted Rachel. This man (Jacob) was married and was seeking a relationship with me. I could not understand how he could be married and think so little of his wife. How could he disrespect his wife, his self, his marriage, and the Father? Why did he make the vow if he was not going to keep it? Was this man (Jacob) only married to his wife to make her happy? Was it out of convenience? Was it because their life of intimacy was over or had too many problems? This man (Jacob) said that I would be his wife. That we would have a family together. This man (Jacob) was seeking to be in a relationship with me. I soon realized something. If I was to become his wife (Rachel) upon him leaving (Leah), what he was doing to his wife would eventually be done to me. I did not want that to happen so I had to move on.

Scenario 3. Leah wanted Jacob's love. I was Leah that wanted to be seen and loved by Jacob. I would do everything within my power to make the man feel special. Trying to get his attention in a way that he would see me and consider the fact that I loved him. I wanted him to see that my love was all he needed. Whatever I thought he would like, would make him happy, and would show him that I was faithful to him, I would do. I was trying to show him that I was worth keeping. Show him that I thought he was important. Why did I feel that I had to prove myself to him? I did it all, hoping that the man would finally see me, want me, and love me. I learned that what I thought was perfection of an amazing woman for him and to him, was not perfection in his thinking. Ultimately, how was I going to keep him happy? I would not have been able to do that, I would have been miserable. How was I going to be happy ever in this relationship? You cannot bring happiness to someone else and you are not happy yourself.

Scenario 4. Rachel was second to Leah. I was Rachel that was second to Leah, that was involved with Jacob. The man was already involved in a relationship with a woman that was the primary woman in his life and I was the second. You may call it side chick, leftovers, second best and I am sure there are other names, I was thinking maybe this relationship was going to work out. I did not have the man to myself, I was sharing him and many a nights and lonely because of it. Listening and believing everything this man was saying to me, while all along he had no intentions of leaving Leah for me. I was so gullible. Leah had children with Jacob and I had nothing. Having children with a man does not mean he is staying with you or loves you. I was trying to have a family with this man, but I was only and always going to be second. I was loved, but was second. I was so jealous of Leah because I felt that she could give him something I could not.

Scenario 5. Leah was married to Jacob, but Jacob was working and doing whatever was necessary to make Rachel his wife. I was Leah, who was in a relationship with a man that I was in love with, yet this man worked hard, longer hours to earn more money to spend on several Rachel's without my knowledge. Here I believed that I was the only one in his life and I was devastatingly mistaken. I was even introduced to them. This Jacob would introduce some of them as acquaintances, or family friends. The crazy part is that some of the women knew they were Rachels and went along with this man's (Jacob) scheme.

Scenario 6. Rachel's beauty compared to Leah. I was a Leah to some men, at least I felt like it. When the man left me to be with another woman, she was always a real nice looking lady and I would compare myself to her. My self-esteem was flushed in the toilet. I would try to immediately go on a diet, get in the gym. I would go and get my hair, nails, and feet done. It was short-lived because I was going to stop all of it and start indulging in sweets, television, and totally go in isolation mode. Was it because he left you for another woman? Yes. I had to learn that his leaving had nothing to do with my looks or because I did something wrong. He wanted the change or was looking for something better.

Scenario 7. Leah was married to Jacob, but was not loved. I was in a relationship and I felt so lonely. I was loved with words, not with action and truth. I was the only one not benefiting from the relationship. It was not going to make a difference what I did nice. This Jacob was for himself. Realizing that I was a symbol of security and stability, I was a mother figure. I took care of home and that was all that mattered to him. He was selfish, but to everyone one else, because of his craftiness of how he used his words to express his love for me, he was a great guy. I never would tear down a word he said. I was supportive, but all alone. A harsh reality. Think about it. I am in a relationship with someone, but in the relationship all alone.

I do not know if you, the reader, have been one of these characters, or if you can relate to my scenarios. All the scenarios developed baggage in my life, like I needed any more than what I already had. I have asked God now, at this point in my life, to prepare me for my mate. The mate that God has for me. In praying this prayer, this means that this is not going to happen on my time. It is not going to happen when I say it is going to happen. This is not an instantaneous process. What I asked God to do, takes time, patience, and discipline. It is a process to become the godly woman that he has designed for me to be. I have also asked God to prepare my mate for me. What this time table looks like I do not know, but I trust God.

Chapter 9

I Was Wounded And Creating Baggage

In these relationships that I was walking into, they were going to become baggage, and I did not realize it. I was a wounded person. That is why I say that the relationships were going to become baggage. Wounded people can wound others, when wounded people have not healed from their wounds. They can wound others if they have not recovered from their wounds. They can wound others if they have not received the proper help or taken the necessary steps to get better, then they remain wounded.

For me, where I am now in life, in my opinion, wounded people who are not in a relationship should get healed, delivered, and help before stepping into another relationship. Otherwise, you are going to enter that new relationship with those existing wounds and may very well become the demise of the relationship. To the ones that are in a relationship, take the necessary steps to heal your hurts so that your significant other, spouse, companion, is given the opportunity to see you at your best. A better you, a healed and delivered you! The wounded just need to admit that they need help in order to move towards the healing process. Who in your life do you admit to that you need help? You can admit to yourself and to God. Everything starts with prayer. The healing process comes through _prayer_. In prayer, you're asking God for help and direction. You are giving your life to God and trusting that God will fix it. If you are wounded and reading this book, this is my prayer for you, that you save yourself and/or the relationship you're involved in with that special person in your life.

Save the relationship by getting help. Love yourself enough to get help for yourself.

The separations from these relationships were unhealthy. Baggage to more baggage, I was taking baggage from one relationship to the next relationship. I was emotionally homeless and an emotional vagabond. It was a domino effect that I did not understood at the time it was occurring. I was simply making things worse. I was looking for love in all the wrong places, just looking for love. This had me running away from God and back to God when the relationships fell apart. What do you mean when you say that you were running away from God? What I mean by that is that I felt I could handle the relationship on my own. I felt like I knew what I was doing and did not need God's help at the time. Now, do you understand what I mean? It was going to go bad, the relationship, and when it did, I would fall apart, and run to God and want a quick fix. God knew my song by heart. You may have learned this depressing song at least once in your life. It is called, "Why Me?" All the tears I have shed, crying to God, wondering when was this going to stop happening to me. My relational problems were not only in my personal life. The relationships with my parents, family members, and friends over the years had problems as well.

I would go to God in prayer about the problems I was having. Sometimes the problems weighed so heavy on my heart. I needed a solution and I needed it fast. One Sunday, at church my pastor said, "When you love expect to get hurt."

What he said was so true. Thank God I got through those problems. People must have been praying for me. And people have been praying for you long before you got here. People were, and are, praying blessings and protection over your life that allowed you to come out of situations. God not only hears those prayers, but He answers. He answered prayers whether it was my grandmother, grandfather, pastor, friend of family, cousin, sister, or brother. The prayers of the righteous availeth much. I just thank God that my name was in the atmosphere and I was being lifted up in prayer.

Relationships were not successful for me. I needed to have a relationship with the Father first. That was the major problem. I think that trying to be in a relationship, and hurting from the first relationship that was so important for a little girl to have, set me up initially for failure. I wonder if not having my first covering of a dad, prevented me from searching out the Father? The very first man that a girl should have a relationship with should have been the first man in her life, which is her father. The young girl should know what to expect from a man because of her father. What he teaches her is so important for her life. She should have something to go by. She should know the difference between a man with good intentions and bad intentions. She needs to know that no one is perfect. She should know how not to play the blame game. It takes two for the relationship to be successful and two to destroy the relationship.

Her father should be the one that tells his daughter that she is beautiful and smart. He should be the one who takes her on her first date, buys her first diamonds, shows her how to ride a bike, buy her first car. I know that the father, or substitute father, is not always in the scenario and strong and courageous women have done their best to raise women.

A lot of those women have been successful as well. I am just speaking of the important role of a father in a daughter's life. The father not being a positive role model in a daughter's life can create a lot of problems. It is like sending your daughter outside blindfolded and asking her to tell you the colors of the flowers. Life is not a fairytale, even though your daughter is a princess. If you are not careful how you raise her, she could be thinking that when she meets a man, it should be magical, like a fairytale. Please don't allow her mindset to be in just fairytale land. Remember the female is a natural nurturer. She is moved in most cases by her emotions, and men think logically.

We thank God for those women, who were blessed to raise upstanding women in this society, but I can only speak for me. Through these relationships that I got involved in the intentions of the guys were totally different from mine. I was used, abused, and misunderstood. Why was I looking for these Fairytale qualities in men? Why? Because that was all I knew, and I was stuck in this mind-set. The view I had was from a child's perspective. There are always internal alarms going off inside of you when something is not right, and sometimes God will send someone you least expect to give you a message to help you out of the pit you're in. What you have to do is recognize that it is help, accept the help, and you began to come out of the pit.

God always gives us a way of escape. We just have to make the decision, whether we are going to accept the help or not. Unfortunately, we think we can change the person or make the relationship better. Change! You have to have the desire to change. No one can make you change or coach you into changing. This is an option that only you can decide upon.

One of my daughters and I were having a conversation about a young lady lying to herself. She has been involved with a young man for about four years. They are not together as far as the male goes, yet they have a child together. The young lady says she understands that he does not want to be with her, but her actions say different.

The young man had his part in telling her what she wanted to hear, which attributed partially to her actions.

This happens a lot.

> *Dialogue Part I: Do not get mad at me because you created a covenant with me. You thought it was just sex? You thought this was going to be a drive-thru get-your-food and leave? You made it more like a drive by. So now that I have caught feelings, I opened up myself to you, which is all of me and now you expect me to turn myself off, like a snooze button on a alarm clock? You have got to be kidding me! How dare you suggest for me to run off and get involved with someone else after making a blood covenant with you. You want me to move on so you can move to the next victim. When did conquer and destroy become a fun thing to do? My feelings cannot turn off after a bond was created with you. For real? This is not easy for me. I am all*

opened now, an easy read, disgraced, humiliated. Who is going to want me now? I have unnecessary baggage. I will be spending my time and energy talking to the next person about how you broke the covenant. Don't get mad at me. You need to understand the ramifications of your actions. You were deceiving and found pleasure, while I was giving a commitment.

Response to Dialogue 1: *Why does the next person have to be a victim? I am not out to conquer and destroy. You want to bring up covenant, but when I met you that was the furthest thing from your mind. From day one, I was attracted to what I saw, just like you were attracted to me. Initially, there were no boundaries established. The only light that was on was green for go. No was never a part of your vocabulary. You allowed me to do whatever I wanted to do. Yes, I received what you were so willingly to give. You and I both knew that it was wrong, but decided to indulge any way. It was not like we did not know that there were no consequences. It was pure sex from the beginning and now that I have moved on because I had never planned to stay indefinitely, it is a problem? Wow!. You were not marriage material, nor was I looking for a marriage. Now I am the bad person. I think not. How about you being the bad one and taking responsibility for your actions? Please!-Please! Don't play the victim. I did not do anything that you did not want me to do. When you said, "Yes," it happened.*

This can go both ways. Sometimes it is the woman that has the characteristics of the male, but this scenario happens, is what I am trying to explain, especially in the society today where everything goes. As a child of the King, I must be careful. I wonder if anyone notices how people want to corrupt the children of God. It seems as though they are on a mission, to make us fall into a trap so they can tell the world that the children of God are no different from the world or worse. Once we fall, the world laughs at us, but with Christ we can fall, but through Christ we are able to rise back up again.

In the beginning, the young man was in school and trying to get his life on track, but somewhere, he fell off the wagon. His mother stepped in and picked up the pieces for him. Was this a good idea? Let us see. I can understand the mother helping out, but to take over was not going to be in the best interest of anyone, especially her son. The mother began making the decisions for him concerning his child, her grandchild, and the young lady went along with it to keep the peace. The mother had taken on the place of the father and the young lady remained in the relationship. However, the mother caused a whole lot of stress. Why was this happening? The young man was a momma's boy. She was crippling this young man. Did she realize it? That I do not know. For a short time, the young man went back to school,and, for whatever reasons, was no longer attending school anywhere; nor did he get a job.

The child is over three years old and the father has not gotten a job, but the young lady has worked and been attending school the entire time. My daughter told me that she expressed to the young lady that she did not want to hear about this situation anymore. My daughter said that this was too much drama and the young lady was just too nice. My daughter was so irritated that the young lady was just allowing herself to be walked all over, and it was not healthy. After all, the young lady birthed this child. I explained to my daughter that she is not sick and tired of the situation, and even though the young man does not want to be with her, she is still holding on. She is somehow hoping things will turn themselves around. It does not take a rocket scientist to figure this out. I told my daughter not to get involved. It is best to stay neutral, because her advice was going to go on deaf ears with the young lady. When a person is tired, or sick and tired of being tired, then comes the change. She is not through emotionally, and until she gets there, no matter how bad things get, she is going to stay right there. Just pray for the young lady. Let me say this again, nothing will change unless you choose for it to change. Change brings about change.

Chapter 10

Keep Your Legs Closed

One day, I remember my grandfather coming by to visit me. He said, "Kim, I want to talk to you."

"Okay," I replied.

"Let's take a walk," he said.

My grandfather was visiting my mother and I at my mother's apartment. My mother lived in this huge apartment complex that had three floors. We lived on the second floor of the building and, in order to walk outside on the sidewalk, you had to go down two flights of stairs and out the security door from our apartment. At the time, my grandfather was saying, "Let's take a walk," we were inside the apartment.

My grandfather was not this big tall man. He was about 5'4 or 5'5 in height. He was a dark-skinned man with blue eyes. He was always well groomed, wore his hair cut low, and I will say he was slender. My grandfather was a family man as I explained earlier in the book, when I told you I had to make a choice between my grandfather and my uncle giving me away at my wedding. He was a hard worker, a great provider for his family, He would joke a lot during family time. A man of few words, he did not like to argue. He was always respectful, but when he wanted to talk, he made his point. When he meant business, he meant business.

We started walking down the street. "Kim, I do not want you to be sleeping around with guys."

My head was straight ahead and my eyes bulged so big, they could have popped out of my head. I was not expecting my grandfather to be having this kind of conversation with me. Where was this coming from? He was not having this conversation with me and my female cousins, just me. I am being singled out. Why? Who told my grandfather what was going on in my life? I believe God sent my grandfather to help me. My grandfather continued to talk to me. He said, "A lot of guys are going to come in your life. All types of guys, but I want you to keep your legs closed. The guy can wait, you hear me?"

"Yes, Granddaddy, I hear you," I said. I felt like if my granddaddy is having this conversation with me, somebody must have told him that my life was getting way out of control. My dad never had this type of conversation with me. I was glad that my grandfather loved me enough to tell me the truth. My grandfather was a family man, a hardworking man, that joked around, enjoyed life, a people person. He was a man of few words, but when he opened his mouth it was serious business.

My grandfather said that I was going to discover from keeping my legs closed, which guys will like me for me and the guys that are there for my body. He explained to me that the man that cares for me will wait for me. He will respect me as a woman and will respect my wishes. He will have good intentions towards me, and if the relationship works out, he will marry me. He told me that opening my legs is not necessary to get what I want. I appreciated my grandfather for having this conversation with me.

I got warnings and alarms that went off inside of me saying, RED ALERT! RED ALERT! PITFALL! PITFALL! NO! NO! but I chose not to listen at times, or I did what you call, partially listen. I had the selective hearing syndrome.

Eventually, things were going to come to a head. My last relationship before I got married, wore me out. I was just tired. I felt as if I had gone twelve rounds in a boxing match. I am not speaking of physical abuse. I am talking about emotional abuse and exhaustion.

I should have listened to my grandfather. I was warned. When we do not take heed to warnings, we leave ourselves open to disaster, harm, and danger.

> *I write not these things to shame you, but as my beloved sons, I warn you.*
>
> —1Corinthians 4:14(KJV)

Chapter 11

Brother On Fire

My dad has a good friend whom I will call Brother-On-Fire. His name really is who he is; a man on fire for the Lord. Brother-On-Fire used to be in the streets with my dad. When I used to visit my dad in the streets, they lived in the hobo camp. Brother-On-Fire, as well as others, lived out there as well. What I have learned recently is that when God has you on an assignment, a mission for Him, He does not always give us explicit details. For example, my assignment was my dad. I assumed it was just my dad. Although, I was praying for my dad to be delivered, set free from his drug addiction, and to come off of the streets, there was something else happening in the process. The men and women living in the hobo camp were watching and listening. I would have conversations with them, never looking down on them, or judging them. I treated them like I would have treated anyone else, with respect. Because of obedience, God was working on the other people while I was on my assignment for my Dad, and a total of seven to eight souls came off the streets and are on fire for the Lord. Brother-On-Fire came out of the streets about a year after my Dad did. He, as well as the seven to eight others, are clean and sober, living for the Lord. God restored Brother-On-Fire's relationships with his family and renewed his youth like the eagles.

You would never think that he lived in the streets, nor my Dad, for that matter. You cannot guess their past by looking at them. When God does something, he does it well. God will clean up what we mess up, or what the devil messes up. He will start our life over again. We become a new creation. God has blessed Brother-On-Fire. God helped him to give sound advice to one of his children. For example, one day his daughter brought a young man to meet him that she was into. I believe, if I am not mistaken, that they were saying they were going to marry.

Brother-On-Fire pulled his daughter aside and asked her was she married yet.

The daughter said, "No, Dad, we are not married."

He then said, "It makes no since to spend money on a wedding, if you are already married. I will spend the money on a wedding. You can have the ceremony, and everyone you want to invite to come. This is only if you are not married, however, if you are married, then it is no since in me spending my money."

When Brother-on-Fire met the young man, he proceeded to ask the question, "Are you two married yet?

The young man was puzzled. "No."

I can only imagine in my mind the look that the young man had to have had on his face, I bet it was priceless.

"Okay," Brother-On-Fire said. He knew that the young man was going to inquire from his daughter what her Dad was talking about. The young man probably thought he was crazy.

Needless to say, the young man asked Brother-on-Fire's daughter. She explained to the young man that her Dad was saying that, if they had slept together, that meant that they were already married. They had consummated the marriage. After hearing that, the young man fled, so we have an idea of what he may have been after. I wish my Dad had been there for me like that, during those young adult years.

While raising my daughters, I told my daughters that if they remained a virgin until marriage, that I would help them have the wedding they wanted, if they waited. I never wanted my daughters to be a statistic of the society in which we live in, where having sex before marriage is today's normality. I was over protective of my daughters because of my life. When did sin become the right thing to do and when did doing good become the bad thing to do? I tell you when; it is everytime we step out of the will of God. My ex-husband and I drilled in their heads the importance of staying pure. That is not to say that they were not going to go contrary to the way we were teaching them.

My children have choices, true, but the choice they make will be knowing the right way to do things, and for them not to do things the right way, is not because we did not teach them what is right. The reality is they have to deal with the consequences: good or bad. As a parent, I could only hope and pray for the best, that they had the eyes to see and the ears to hear. Lord, give them a listening spirit. I did not want my children to have to deal with the bad consequences.

When you think about all the possible scenarios that could have possibly happened as a result of doing things the wrong way, that alone was the thriving force that kept me watching and talking to my children. It was important to me that I had a relationship with my children where communication was not a problem. There are too many children talking to other children. Children involved in things and the parents have no clue as to what is going on for a lack of communication.

I was so emotionally exhausted, like I said earlier from the relationship before my marriage. I began to pray to God to send me a man that respected me and my wishes. Someone that would be willing to wait to have sex after marriage, not before. I had to teach my girls the right way to live, knowing the consequences that can happen if they choose to go contrary to the way they were brought up. I would not love them any less.

In the next chapter, you will read about the Chameleon. Once I got involved with the Chameleon, I stepped into the arena of sin and when you step into the arena of sin it is an arena of several addictions. Once you yield to the addictions, you are in trouble. What's in the sin arena that is addictive? In the arena, there is wrath, anger, evil desires, slanderers, immoral behavior, impurity, gossipers, greed, liars, unbelief, and more. The sin arena is nothing to play with. It is a day-by-day process to stay away from the arena as a believer. I got caught up in the sin arena too many times so let's read what happened to me when I entered the arena with the Chameleon.

Chapter 12

I Was Stuck On Stupid With The Chameleon

When it comes to dating, people should really take the time to get to know the person of interest. It is important not to rush the process; you may miss some vital and useful details. I am saying this because it cost me when I did not take the time out to get to know who I was dating. I was surface dating. Surface is the outer part or uppermost layer of something. The surface is the, outer, outside, outermost, outward, external part of a person. In order to get to know someone we need to get to as much of the internal part of a person as possible. This is a timely process in order to accomplish this task. I am going to describe the surface of this character and tell you what happened as a result of me getting to know the surface of the man.

I am going to refer to this character as the Chameleon. I call this character the Chameleon because I came to learn years later that he would change up women like you change your underwear. Chameleon even changed my name. I could never get him to call me by my name. He would call me Kimala. I remember telling him my name is Kim. "Call me Kim," but he would say he knows what my name is, but he was going to call me Kimala. I recently decided to look up the name to see what it meant. To my surprise it was better than I could have imagined. The name means extremes in fortune, health and spirituality.

On one website, it said, "You are very versatile, idealistic, and intuitive. You either enjoy great success or abject misery. The solution is service to others. Use your leadership abilities for humanity and not for self-glorification. You are intuitive and might be interested in the arts, drama, or science. You are always looking for an opportunity to achieve financial and emotional security. You are basically peacemaker. You understand the law of harmony and desire to balance your life with those around you. You may feel incomplete without someone to share your love, ideals, wealth, or work. You can be very sensitive and could appear a bit shy and perceptive. You have developed intuition, patience and the ability to nurture others. You can achieve the state of happiness if you are willing to accept your needs in a complimentary relationship and go to create them."

On a different website, it said, "The meaning of Kimala is Anointed, Follower of Christ."

What a meaning of a name. I am absolutely amazed that all these years, Chameleon called me this, and I did not even know what the name meant. Thank you, Jesus, it was not an evil name that he was so adamant about calling me. I met the Chameleon at a local skating rink that I regularly went to weekly. I was getting ready to leave the skating rink. I was sitting down taking my skates off, and he introduced himself. He gave me his number to call him and asked me could he have my number to call me. I did not feel like it was any harm in doing that so I gave him my number. Chameleon was very persistent come to think about it. He asked me did I need a ride home.

When I told him that I did not need a ride home, he told me that he was not driving a bucket, he was driving a BMW. I looked at him and said, "So?" I still do not need a ride home. I am not a materialistic person, so I was not impressed by the type of car that he said he drove.

"Just because a person is driving a BMW does not mean that they own the BMW."

"Why do you say that, Kim?"

Because he did not own the BMW, which I soon found out. I believe his interpretation for BMW was that it stood for, "Brings More Women." You still have some women today that are attracted to men who appear to have material wealth. Everything that looks real is not the real truth.

When I got home from the skating rink, I had not been in the house 20 minutes. and my phone rings. It was late. Who could have been calling me after 10:00 p.m.? I answered the phone and it was Chameleon. He started the conversation off with an apology for calling me so late. He explained to me that he just wanted to make sure I gave him the correct number.

He proceeded to say that he was going to let me go, but he wanted to know if I would go out with him the following Friday night. I told him sure. I was thinking to myself that this was different. The Chameleon was tall golden brown and handsome. He was 6'6, slender, smooth caramel complexion, green eyes that changed with whatever color he wore, a nice smile. He was confident, had a great sense of humor, and charismatic. He said that he was a Christian, but what type was he? The first date lead to many dates. We had been dating for about six months. He seemed to be the perfect gentleman and I liked him a lot. I had my first apartment that I had recently moved in a couple of months before I met Chameleon. I was starting to believe that I had literally hit the jackpot. I had my own place and now a great guy, so I thought.

Finally, there would be no more dating for me. I have someone in my life that truly likes, cares for me, and he's a Christian. I got too comfortable too quick. I gave Chameleon a key to my apartment so that when he worked a split shift on his job he could come by and rest at my place. Needless to say, he was very pleased with my decision to give him a key to my place. I am sure if he was not quite sure how I felt about him, it was all clear when he got the key. One day, Chameleon asked me if I wanted to go watch him bowl because he was going to sub for another player on a bowling league team. I told him that that was fine. On the way to go he needed to stop by one of his brother's house first. I did not mind. He wanted me to meet his family because he wanted his family to know who his lady was in his life, so he claimed. When we arrived to the brother's house, we went into the house and he immediately started to introduce me to the family members there.

All of the members that were at the house were apparently waiting on him to arrive so that they could all leave together at the same time to the bowling alley. It was two brothers, one brother's girlfriend, and a sister-n-law that was going. One of the brothers looked a little agitated when he saw me. He walked over to where Chameleon and I were standing and said, "Excuse me." He told Chameleon that he needed to talk to him. I was curious about what was discussed because I felt a sense of displacement. I was no longer comfortable. I knew something was wrong. When we got in the car, he was trying to act like everything was okay, but I was not buying that. I asked him was everything okay, knowing that whatever was said between him and his brother was very unsettling.

He said, "Yes," with a smile. I asked him did I offend his brother, say, or do something wrong? I wanted to get to the bottom of it. The vibe was different and he was trying his best to cover it up. He told me no, so I decided to just leave it alone. I think that I was very naïve. I had warning signs that I simply overlooked. We spent a lot of time together and I would have never suspected that he was cheating. When I look back to those times, in overlooking the warning signs, it lead me to a lot of unnecessary heartache. I was young, not perfect, and was entering into a costly life lesson. Who wants to see the bad in someone they like? I do not believe that people generally look for the bad in someone. They want to see the good in the people they love and care about.

Everything happens for a reason. Some reasons are for your own good, and you do not even realize it. Shortly after I had given Chameleon the key, my mother came to live with me for awhile. By my mother living with me that meant that he had to return my key and he could not spend the night, nor come over when he pleased. I was not seeing him as often because of this. Things were about to take a drastic turn for the worst. Chameleon was changing. That is what a chameleon does. The chameleon has the ability to change color. They can look in two directions at once. It is called rotating their focus to observe two different objects at the same time, which allows them to move their eyes independently from each other.

The change in color can occur in as little as 20 seconds. They are born with special cells that have color or pigment in them. These cells lie in layers under the outer skin. Many people think that the chameleons change to blend with their surroundings, but scientists' studies show that light, temperature and mood cause them to change color. Sometimes changing color makes them more comfortable or helps them communicate with other chameleons. The chameleon had more than one agenda going on at the same time. I was going to learn that he was going to change and the reason for the change was to communicate with other women. Even though he was changing he was suppose to blend in such a way that I would not think that he was being deceptive. He was distant and always busy.

Kim, you say he was changing, but if he was seeing multiple women, don't you think he was doing that before you? Yes, of course he was, but when I speak of change, I am speaking from the way the relationship started. The man he was initially to me changed. He purchased two pagers and had a cell phone. You are probably saying to yourself, a pager? That was so long ago. It was not in the dinosaur's age, but they existed.

I remember asking Chameleon why he felt the need to have two pagers. He told me one was for family and friends and the other was for work. This was so that he could keep business calls and family calls separate. I accepted the answer, but I was going to eventually find out it was a lie. I went from seeing him five to six days a week, to two or three times every week. This did not bother me at first because he was still coming to see me. When he did not make time to spend quality time, a red flag went off in my head. Chameleon met my family and close friends. In the beginning everyone liked him. They had no reason to dislike him. He was very sociable and a joy to be around.

A year had passed and things seemed to be going well between us. One Friday, February 2, 1990 early evening I was at home. Chameleon gave me a call to see how I was doing. I was home alone and he made the statement that he was going to go hang out with some of his boys late that evening about ten o'clock. He wanted to come and see me and spend a little time with me. I told him that I would love to see him. When he arrived, he wanted to be intimate and we were. Chameleon was telling me that he wanted me to have his child. I told him that, that could not happen now. I told him that I wanted to wait until I was married first, then a baby would be fine.

Little did I know, I got pregnant that night. Oh, foolish one I was—in the heat of the moment—no protection was not smart.

If you do not use protection, then this is one of the possible consequences of this action. Before he left I asked him if I was going to see him on Sunday and he said yes. Chameleon left and I looked forward to seeing him on Sunday evening. Sunday evenings were the nights we met up at the skating rink. Sunday evening came and I was about to receive some horrible news. I arrived at the skating rink and started looking for him. One of his brothers and one of his sisters hung out on Sunday evening as well. I saw them and decided to say hello. I thought to myself, I will ask them where Chameleon was. I asked his sister was he on his way. She called over her brother closer to where we were standing. I repeated the question. They had a complete look of shock on their faces, like I had asked them the wrong question.

I asked again, his brother said, "I don't believe this! She does not know!"

His sister said, "He is a dirty dog! Girl, he got married yesterday."

What a blow! I was looking with disbelief.

His brother said, "I told him to tell you the truth when I first met you the night we went bowling, and to leave you alone."

"I can't begin to describe how and what I was feeling at that moment. They could not be serious. The brother and sister had a few choice words of expression about their brother and the cruelty that was done to me. They both apologized to me, for their brother, but this was not their fault. I immediately got my things and left the skating rink. It took me all night and half of the next day to really process all of this before, I completely broke down. It was Monday mid-afternoon and my phone rings. I answer the phone and it is Chameleon, unbelievable! I should have hung up in his face. I asked him why he was calling me. I told him that he was suppose to be on his honeymoon with his wife. I said this so that he would know that I found out that he got married. I was so furious and disgusted. I told him that he made his choice and not to call my number again. "Lose my number!"I exclaimed. "You are a married man and I do not mess with married men." He had the audacity to tell me that he loved me and that he was going to get an annulment. I hung up the phone in his face. Three or four weeks went by, and he calls me again.

I guess he thought that it would take three or four weeks to cool down. I said, "Didn't I tell you to lose my number?" I hung the phone up in his face again.

He called me right back and said, "Kimala, I am sorry. I made a mistake. This had been planned two years ago, and I did not know what to do, but I love you."

My reply was, "If you loved me, you would have never gotten married."

He said, "We are getting the marriage annulled. I do not want to be with her. I want to be with you." He then asked me, "-Are you pregnant?"

I said, "No! I am not pregnant."

He said, "Yes, you are because I have been sick as a dog."

"Maybe you had some bad food or you are catching the flu," I said. This was something I did not need to happen.

He said, "No, I told you I was going to get you pregnant. You are, and it is going to be a girl!" I told him.

"I am not the one sick, so you are mistaken." I got off the phone. When I got off the phone, I realized that I had not had a menstrual cycle, but this was not the first time that I missed a cycle. The doctor gave me a shot for it to start. To prove him wrong, I decided to go and get a pregnancy test anyway. I took the test, and it was positive. Oh, my God!

I cried, "A baby, no husband, wow!"

I needed to get over this man, get him completely out of my system, but how was I going to do that now? A couple of weeks later he called me and said that he and his wife got the marriage annulled. He then proceeded to say, "You are pregnant right? You found out that you are having my baby right?"

I hesitated before answering him. I told him, "Yes, I did find out that I was pregnant.

"It's a girl," he said.

"You do not know what it is," I said, "and I want you to stay away from me.

Go be with your wife." He said that the marriage is annulled and I am staying with my sister. It just happened to be a sister that I had not met. How convenient. How was I going to verify what he was saying was true or not true? I took him back. He apologized for hurting me. He told me that we would get married. He went so far as to ask my family for my hand in marriage. I remember the day that he told my grandparents that he wanted to marry me. My grandmother looked him in the eyes and said, "I hope you mean what you say. My grandmother told him that people that do not do right by the people in this family, no good comes of them.

She said, "I do not know why that is, but if you say you are going to marry our granddaughter, I hope you are being truthful."

Well, he was just talking. He really did not listen to what my grandmother said. Things were going in the wrong direction fast. The signs of deception were obvious, but I was steady ignoring the signs. I asked Chameleon why he felt the need to wear the two pagers, plus a cell phone. Why did I ask him? What made me think that he was really going to tell me the truth? Chameleon said that one pager was for work and one pager was for everyone else. I began to see less of him. Six months into my pregnancy, Chameleon came by to see me and told me that a girl at his job was saying that she was pregnant by him.

All bad, is all I can say. He continued the conversation by telling me that the girl had been sexually active with not only him, but two other guys at the job and he did not believe it was his. What kind of mess was I involved in? This man was not using protection, nor are the other parties involved. This was being irresponsible and negligent on everybody's part. Chameleon was not only jeopardizing his health, but jeopardizing the health of all parties and possibly two unborn children. The question was, at this point, was I becoming numb to his behavior? Was my self-esteem so low that I accepted this behavior from him? Was I trying to make things work because a baby was involved now? As the months progressed, Chameleon began fooling around with many women. He was such a man whore.

He was having such a good time that he decided to tell me that he did not want to get married. He was not ready for marriage, he said; he just wanted to fool around with other women. This man told me that he should have been a porn star. He was out of control! Even though he did not want to get married, he would be here for the baby, he mentioned. I appreciated the honesty from him about wanting to be with other women and not wanting to get married, but was this a form of reverse psychology? Was he really trying to cover up lies that he was telling to justify his present and future actions? Well, it's true he was lying to me. Chameleon was still married; he never got an annulment.

What about Chameleon's wife? Did she ever find out about you? Yes, I had had enough. I knew how to get in contact with his wife and that is what I did. Once I contacted his wife, I told her my name because she did not know who I was. I explained to her that I had been seeing her husband, believing that their marriage was annulled.

Upon finding out that this was false information, I asked that she would keep her husband away from me. The response was interesting. She proceeded to say, "Girl, men do that all the time, but he is coming home to me at the end of the day."

I responded, "That's fine."

"I just want you to keep him away from me. That is all I ask."

The phone conversation ended.

We did not argue, nor yell on the phone. I got my point across, which was all that I wanted to do. I assumed that speaking to her would keep him away from me. This was not so. This was ridiculous.

Chameleon called me that night. "You called my wife?"

"YES, because you did not get the message. Leave me alone." This was the same individual that said his marriage was annulled.

He repeats himself again, "My wife, Kim?"

I replied, "I sure did. You are a liar. Leave me alone!"

He said, "Okay, I am going to get you for that."

I hung up the phone. Immediately, I decided to call the police department to tell them that I was pregnant and he had threatened me.

The police came by my house and took my statement and made a police report. The police also made a suggestion for me to get a restraining order. I went to file a restraining order and requested that the sheriffs serve him at his job. It was like he knew that he was going to be served. He was avoiding every way possible from getting served. It took three attempts then he was served. Do you think that was the end? Do you think that closed that chapter of my life with the Chameleon? The answer is no. He called me and told me that the restraining order was not going to keep him away from me. He told me that his intentions were not to hurt or harm me. I thought to myself that this man is crazy! I needed to protect myself, so I changed my job location and my phone number.

This man still found me. I was working one day at my new job site. It was a nice day. Everything was going smooth at the job. I was asked to go to the supply room to get a product for my boss's client. Another hairstylist came to the supply room where I was. "Kim, there is a man up front in the waiting area here to see you."

I told the other hairstylist that nobody knows that I work here.

She said, "Girl, this man asked for you by your full name, he brought flowers, and he is fine."

"Come out. I will get the product. You go up front. He seems like a nice man."

I told her okay, but I was trying to run through my thoughts, trying to figure out who this could be. The hairstylist took the product from me and gave it to my boss, when she noticed that I was still in the back, she came back to the supply room.

"Girl, come on don't keep him waiting."

I asked her, "What does he look like because nobody knows that I work here.

She said, "Girl, he is tall, caramel complexion, green eyes, he is fine."

I was thinking, *No, No, No,* in my head, *this cannot be happening right now.* How did this man find me? This was so disturbing and scary. This was a new job, and I definitely did not want to have drama at my job, and most certainly did not want these people at my job in my personal business. I walked to the front and yes, it was Chameleon. Lord, help me! I suggested we go outside and talk. When we got outside away from listening ears, I asked him how he found me. I asked him did he have someone watching me. He told me that he has his ways. I told him that this was stalking, he was stalking me.

This man told me that he was not going anywhere. I was carrying his baby, and that meant I would always have a part of him. How is it that I fell for this nutcase? I stayed in communication with this guy that I could not seem to get rid of. I hoped that out of all this that he would at least be a good father to the unborn child. I knew he could not be trusted to be in a committed relationship with me, much less anyone else. When the child was born, he was there. He kept his promise to be there when the child was born. I felt that he was not going to fulfill his promise to take care of this child, due to his lifestyle. One day I was running low on diapers and formula, and I could not get to the store. I called him and asked him if he would go by the store when he got off from work and purchase the items for me, then bring them by the house. I only needed enough to last me two weeks.

Chameleon did not come that evening or the next morning. I remember him calling me like everything was wonderful. I politely said, "I asked you if you could go and purchase some diapers and formula and you did not come through." He began to interrupt and apologize. I peacefully said, "No, let me finish. I will never deny you to see your child. I will not fill your child's head with negative things about you. I want her to see you for who you are. It is up to you to build a relationship with your child, but you will never have to worry about me asking you to buy another thing ever."

I kept that promise. I put myself in that mess, and I did not know how to get myself out. It is not like I was really going in blind. When your gut is telling you something is wrong, and you do not listen, it is on you. As people, we want what we want and even when we know the truth, we know someone or something is not good for us we get into self and think that we can fix it, make it better. If something or someone is not for me or is unhealthy for me, I want to be ridden of it so I can move on to better. I was sinking deeper in a ditch with the Chameleon, but it was unhealthy. No one deserves to be mistreated or used, and I kept allowing it to continue. Shame on me. Once I realized I was incapable of getting out of the relationship with him, I ran from this relationship into a marriage.

No down time, no airing out. I remember on my wedding day, I received a call from the Chameleon and he told me that I was making a big mistake, just because I am angry with him, does not mean I should get married. This is the worst mistake to make. He felt that I was rushing him into marriage. He wanted to date for awhile, then get married. I could not trust him as far as I could see him. That means if he is standing right in front of me I could not trust him, I explained to him. I hung up the phone and went to get married.

Was the Chameleon right about the marriage? Yes, he was right, you do not run from one relationship into another, but I could not get him out of my system. I was stuck on stupid with the Chameleon.

Chapter 13

Not Equipped For Marriage

Did I get married? Yes, I did get married. My marriage started off with a lie and a way of escape from a previous relationship. If you start off a relationship with a lie it is not going to work. Whether you lie to the other person or to yourself, it is still a lie. We must understand that anything built on lies is going to not only be detrimental to you but to the other person. If you are running from one relationship and into the next, you have decided to have a life spent on the run, Running from situations, instead of solving them. You need to find out your purpose in life, figure out what you learned from the relationship, before moving forward. It is important to face any situation head on. I was married for eighteen years. Before I got married, I was in no way equipped, much less ready for marriage to anyone. I was that classic case of, "Everybody is getting married and I am all alone."

I figured I was on that late train and I was going to miss out. All the alarms were going off and I truly did not take heed to any of them. When you do not listen, it cost you. Marriage is sacred and should not be taken lightly.

You really need to understand marriage before entering into it. It is also important for you to get to know who you are before marriage. I did not mention your mate. I said, "Get To Know You First." We perish for a lack of knowledge, and we also perish especially, for not listening, when God is trying to get a message to us. God is still the same God today as He was yesterday. The God who knew you and I before the Foundations of the World, which He created.

Listen to advice to advice and accept discipline, and at the end you will be counted among the wise.
—**Proverbs 19:20 (NIV)**

My sheep listen to my voice; I know them, and they follow me. I give them eternal life,and they shall never perish; no one will snatch them out of my hand.
—**John10:27 (NIV)**

    Marriage was one relationship that I placed no value in. I ran out of the relationship with the Chameleon and into a marriage, as I said before. I felt that I could make the marriage work if I wanted to. It was like a negotiation of a business deal. Who was I trying to convince? I had a form of Godliness. I was a fake. I was trusting in self. I did not study the Word of God. This was where failure lives and dwells, in thinking I could do it by myself. When you are studying the Word of God, well, even reading the Word of God on a consistent basis, it will change your life from a form of Godliness to a life becoming godly by faith. The healing really starts when you can admit the truth about yourself and make the effort to change what is out of order in your life. Remember faith comes by hearing, hearing by the Word of God. In my mind my ex-husband and I both had a position and as long as we fulfilled our individual position, the marriage would be fine. I did not know what was expected from me as a wife, but I did have a view from a child's perspective of marriage. I expected my husband to treat me like I saw my dad treat my mom when I was little. It is what I call the Fairytale view. When you look at a marriage and only see a **Fairytale** view you are in trouble.

    Marriage is not like a Fairytale you make up in your mind and it comes to pass like you envisioned.**Marriage** is more like trying to create the perfect Fairytale that children all over the world would love. This would take a lot of work, a very creative team of individuals to make it happen. Marriage is work between two willing individuals who put God first and understand the covenant they have entered into together before God. Marriage is a covenant relationship that takes work and failing to understand that is titled, <u>Disaster Waiting To Happen.</u> A lot of times people are in love with the wedding production, the ceremony. Some people want to have the ceremony get all dolled up, party, and go on the honeymoon and live in that excitement forever. Some people want the wedding, not the marriage. I had my part in the demise of my marriage. I will not deny that and I have learned some hard lessons behind my part in the demise of my marriage.

When you get married, it is two different individuals that come together to be one flesh. A united front. The two individuals in most cases do not think about the fact they both are carrying their own luggage. In the process of them getting to know one another, some of their individual luggage begins to open and Wow! They notice. They realize that they were not aware of some of the items each other were carrying around in their luggage. One of the largest pieces of luggage one or both of the individuals have is called debt. Get yourself out of debt. Do not hide the fact that you have debt. It is living a lie. Do not start off with lies. Lies destroy. Learn how to be responsible for yourself first. Is it fair to have someone take care of your responsibilities?

Some people are looking for a way out of their debt through another individual. They are marrying to get out of debt, not for love. God weighs the motive of a man and so should we. There are some people who will love them enough to take their debts on. Debts are not always to a creditor; some debts are to others. It is admirable of that individual, but it can create a bigger problem down the road. This could turn the individual into a Mr. Rescue or Ms. Rescue, which can be draining. Getting rid of luggage like this can possibly shortstop the early onset of financial problems between the two individuals, as well as health issues. Learn how to be a good steward over your finances and your responsibilities before jumping into a marriage.

FAIRYTALE VIEW

Are you wondering what I mean by **Fairytale** view? **Fairytale** is place of fantasy or make-believe. It is a perfect place. What a picture to have in my mind, "Right?" I had this picture of my parents' marriage before it went sour. My parents would get a new car every two years.

My brother and I were taken shopping all the time. We had to have school clothes, dress clothes for church, play clothes, summer clothes, and for those special days like Easter. My brother and I shared one of the rooms that was close to my parents' room. We slept on twin beds, but we had anything we wanted. My parents both worked, but my dad's profession is what stood out the most. My dad used to come home and bring my mother gifts just because he loved her and was thinking about her. Dad and Mom laughed, hugged, went out on dates, and it did not have to be a special occasion. I was used to seeing my parents turning on music and dancing with each other. They would be in the family room playing their favorite songs, slow dancing, and I would step in between them to join in the dancing with them. I would have my feet on my Dad's and slow dance with my parents, at least, I thought I was dancing.

I had the best Dad in the world! All my friends liked my dad, and my cousins on both sides of the family loved my dad. They always wanted to come around. Dad was a provider in the house, and we did not want for anything. It was perfect from a child's view at one point. My dad was the man who got the kids together and had everybody playing flag football in the streets, or giving rides to the kids on his personal motorcycle. If my dad was going to buy my brother and I something, and my cousins or friends were around, he would treat them as well. He was a fair man. My mother was a good Mom. She fixed us up when we got hurt, took care of us, the house, and Dad. My parents worked together as a team.

Dad had taken my brother and me horseback riding one day and we enjoyed it so much, Dad asked me if I wanted my very own pony. I told my dad, yes, so he said, "Okay, I am going to get you a pony."

My parents even talked about remodeling the house, putting an upstairs on the house and a swimming pool in the backyard. I thought from a child's perspective I had the perfect life, not knowing what was lurking around the corner for my family.

Chapter 14

They Were Not The Only Ones Divorcing

My world started off the right way and life's surprises changed everything. My parents and I got a divorce and it was the worst divorce ever, at least I thought so. Did you catch what I said? My parents and I got a divorce?

Parents do not realize that if the children are old enough to know that Mom and Dad are no longer together, it affects them, too! The separations and feelings of abandonment started to develop. The perfect world was falling apart, piece by piece. Most couples getting a divorce that have a child or children, get so consumed with the issues they are having with each other, they never stop to consider the effect that it is having on the child or children. It is hard on the children, too!

Let me go to the deep end of the pool, as my pastor says. When you go to church and the pastor/ bishop and his wife are our spiritual mother and father. That means that the pastor/bishop and his wife have children. They have children that are of all ages. They have infant children all the way up to adult children.

The pastor/bishop and his wife teaches, prays for, nurtures, and counsels their children. I am sure the desire is to have all their children to grow up to be spiritually mature adults. Our spiritual parents do not want to let their parent, God, down. They do not want to be held responsible for misleading their children. They try to make sure that the older children help them and teach the younger siblings what they were taught by them. You see their parent, God anointed them and called them to teach how to live in this world. They are our spiritual parents, not perfect in anyway, but they do their best. We, as spiritual children, look up to our parents.

We expect them to be good examples and not make any mistakes. Again, they are not perfect. They, too, make mistakes.

Allow me to share a story about a pastor whose church I used to attend. I was attending a church and, at the time, this pastor of mine got a divorce. Then the pastor immediately got remarried. The church had not had a chance to process the fact that their parents were divorced. Our spiritual mom was not there and her children were wondering where she was and what happened. The children of the church were affected by the divorce. Some ran away from home out of anger and confusion. Some ran to their spiritual parents' friends' homes. They were looking to be adopted into a new family, not any family, but a good family. Some of the children started bickering with one another. Some of the children felt as though the pastor getting a divorce from his wife gave them grounds to divorce their wives or husbands.

Kim, did you get a divorce because of this pastor? No, I did not get a divorce because of that situation and my divorce was about ten years later. I only remember a few close pastors that came and prayed for us as a church, but it seemed like the prayer was more so for our pastor and his new wife.

We needed counseling and healing as a church, which could not happen overnight. Some of the children stayed with the pastor because of their love for him. Did you stay? Yes, I stayed for a while, but my family found a new church home eventually. Children were trying to figure out where this woman came from. Who is she? We now have to call her Mother? We already have a mother. Why were the children not informed prior to the marriage? Why were the children not invited to the wedding?

I remember being told, touch not my anointed and do my prophet no harm. Why was that being said? We did not want to hurt our spiritual father; we loved him. The pastor may have felt like his personal life had nothing to do with his spiritual family.

Is there a difference between the two? Accountability is accountability, right? The spiritual father tried to explain to us what was going on, the best he could, I believe, but for every action, there is a reaction. Some children just could not get over the divorce. The pastor was called and anointed by God, and he is still doing God's work. I love that pastor and I still pray for him and his present wife. I just wanted to give you an example, so back to what I was saying.

If your child or children are old enough to realize what is happening. Never underestimate the child or children's understanding of what is happening around them.

Some parents going through a divorce use the child or children as pawn pieces in a chess game.

Some adults can be very selfish people, especially from a child's view. The child is always in the background crying out, what about me? Whether it is through disobedience, trying to receive more affection, or isolation to get the parents attention. The adults dated each other, they fell in love with each other, they got married, they had children, they basically did what they wanted to do. The beginning always seems magical. The couple says we can do this together; and when the relationship starts to go sour, it turns into, "I can't stand you," "It's all your fault," "I hate you," "You never listen," and they are ready to bail out.

Hello? You are forgetting about the children! Some adults feel like children do not understand what is going on and sometimes children do not, but it affects them in more ways than anyone can imagine. What about the children that blame themselves for the breakup of their family?

The children become a possession, a volleyball between the couple, and while they are fighting, trying to destroy each other, they are destroying the children. I am not speaking for the abusive relationships. The abused individual needs to get away from the abuser. A relationship like that can destroy children as well. The memories of a child affects their lives, the rest of their life. If they do not get any healing for those deep scars they suffered from the divorce it can be detrimental to their future. Most adults never even look back to consider the children, much less survey the damages because they feel their divorce is about them and not the children. The imprint we as the parents leave on a child's mind can affect them the rest of their lives, they will definitely make some life decisions based on their parents' relationships. With my dad out of the house, I was being divorced too. I was a gift, a blessing that came out of the covenant that my parents made. I was now unprotected, no covering. A covering is important, and I didn't have it anymore.

> *Now the serpent was craftier than any of the wild animals the Lord God had made. He said to the woman, "Did God really say, "You must not eat from any tree in the garden?" The woman said to the serpent, We may eat fruit from the trees in the garden, but God did say, "You must not eat fruit from the tree in the middle of the garden, and you must not touch it, or you will die."*
> **—Genesis 3:1-3, (NIV)**

Eve's covering, which was Adam, was not protecting her from the craftiness of the serpent. With Adam not acting as her covering, it left her susceptible to the enemy. The enemy was able to play on words to trip Eve up, to deceive her. She even lied as well. The man is the Head of the Household, the covering for his family. My dad was out of the household and I was not covered. Looking for my dad, when I should have been looking to the Father. When it came to relationships, I had it backwards.

> *"The Lord God said, "It is not good for man to be alone. I will make a helper suitable for him."*
> **—Genesis 2:18, (NIV)**

> *"He who finds a wife finds what is good and receives favor from the Lord"*
> **—Proverbs 18:22, (NIV)**

> *House and wealth are the inheritance from fathers, But a wise understanding and sensible wife is [a gift and a blessing] from the Lord.*
> — **Proverbs 19:14,(AMP)**

When a man of God is seeking God first finds a Godly woman seeking God first, will find a good thing in my opinion.

> *Then the Lord God made a woman from the rib he had taken out of the man, and brought her to the man.*
> —**Genesis 2:22, (NIV)**

Chapter 15

The Woman I Need To Become

The interpretation I get from the passage of scripture that speaks of seeking God first is plain. It means exactly what it says, we should be seeking God first and His kingdom. His way of doing things that he has given us in the Bible. By doing this in this manner it allows God to teach us his ways of doing things. There is nothing new under the sun, and everything we need to know is in the Bible. Are we willing to study to search to find the answers? It would allow God to impart the wisdom needed for the man and the woman. For the woman is to become the virtuous woman stated in Proverbs.

A capable, intelligent and virtuous woman--who is he who can find her? She is far more precious than jewels and her value is far above rubies, or pearls. 11, The heart of her husband trusts in her confidently and relies on and believes in her securely, so that he has no lack of [honest] gain or need of [dishonest] spoil. 12, She comforts, encourages, and does him only good as long as there is life within her. 13, She seeks out wool and flax and works with willing hands [to develop it]. 14, She is like the merchant ships loaded with foodstuffs; she brings her household's food from a far [country]. 15,She rises while it is yet night and gets [spiritual] food for her household and assigns her maids their tasks. 16, She considers a [new] field before she buys or accepts it [expanding prudently and not courting neglect of her present duties by assuming other duties]; with her savings *[of time and strength]* she plants fruitful vines in her vineyard. 17, She girds herself with strength *[spiritual, mental, and physical fitness for her God-given task]* and makes her arms strong and firm. 18, She tastes and sees that her gain from work *[with and for God]* is good, her lamp goes not out, but it burns on continually through the night *[of trouble, privation, sorrow, warning away fear, doubt, and distrust]*. 19, She lays her hands to the spindle, and her hands hold distaff. 20, She opens her hand to the poor, yes, she reaches out her filled hands to the needy *[whether in body mind, or spirit]*. 21, She fears not the snow for her family, for all her household are doubly clothed in scarlet. 22, She makes herself coverlets, cushions, and rugs of tapestry. Her clothing is of linen, pure and fine, and of purple *[such as that of which clothing of the priests and the hallowed cloths of the temple were made]*. 23, Her husband is known in the *[city's]* gates, when he sits among the elders of the land. 24, She makes fine linen garments and leads others to buy them; she delivers to the merchants girdles for sashes that free one up for service. 25, Strength and dignity are her clothing and her position is strong and secure; she rejoices over the future *[the latter day or time to come, knowing that she and her family are in readiness for it]*! 26, She opens her mouth in skillful and godly Wisdom, and on her tongue is the law of kindness *[giving counsel and instruction]*. 27, She looks well to how things go in her household, and the bread of idleness(gossip, discontent, and self-pity) she will not eat. 28, Her children rise up and call her blessed (happy, fortunate, and to be envied); and her husband boasts of and praises her, *[sayings]*. 29, Many daughters have done virtuously, nobly, and well *[with the strength of character that is steadfast in goodness]*, but you excel them all. 30, Charm and grace are deceptive, and beauty is vain [because it is not lasting], but a woman who reverently and worshipfully fears the Lord, she shall be praised! 31, Give her the fruit of her hands and let her own works praise her in the gates [of the city]!

—**Proverbs 31:10-31 (AMP)**

One way I interpret this passage of scripture, is as follows:

1. I must develop the ability to be insightful and a discerning woman.
2. I must be honest with God and with myself.
3. I must be an encourager, be accountable for myself, a comforter , loving and a doer of good deeds.
4. Develop survival skills, nurturing skills, and become one who's behavior becomes a life of holiness.
5. Develop a prayer life and most of all a relationship with Christ
6. I must accept and not neglect my responsibilities in every area of my life.
7. A good steward over my finances, obey the laws of sowing and reaping, tithes and offerings. I must know how to budget my finances, knowing when to spend and when to save.
8. I must take care of my body, mind, and spirit. I must work on keeping myself healthy, fit, and knowledgeable of God's word.
9. I must not become enslaved to anything.
10. I must be careful what I say, set an example and not be a gossiper.

Reading Proverbs 31, I see these attributes of a godly woman and I know for me this would take some time to learn and become. I would not call this an overnight process. During the times before and the times after this was written in the Bible, women probably were trained as a child on up to become the woman of Proverbs 31. When God brought Adam, his wife that God created, in God's image, his wife was equipped to be the perfect suitable helper for Adam. She did not have to compare herself to or compete with any other woman, or feel the need to compete.

She did not have to wonder if he saw her. She did not have to be concerned about other men looking at her or pursuing her, knowing she belonged to Adam. She did not have to worry about Adam turning his head at every woman within his sight. She had no insecurities. I truly wish I had known those things before I started dating and before I got married. Because, as a wife, with a lack of knowledge, I was a partaker in the demise of my very own marriage. There are no fingers to point at anyone when I have four pointing back in my direction. I have to accept what I did wrong and where I went wrong so I can heal. I needed to ask for God's forgiveness and learn from the mistakes I made, so that I never make them again in the future. The battle was not mine; it was the Lord's.

> *The Lord will fight for you, and you shall hold your peace and remain at rest.*
>
> —Exodus 14:14 (AMP)

I have learned that it is my job to study the Word of God to know how I am to live as a woman of God. I have to become saturated in the Word. I am not saying to be overly righteous. There are guidelines that I must follow, so that I am living like God wants me to live. In order to know those guidelines I must read the Bible to be the example of a godly woman to others. The only way to do this is by reading, retaining, and applying it to my life. There are areas of weakness that need to be worked on. I have to make sure that I do not have bitterness and resentment towards others. I need to be a forgiving person. I do not need anything hindering my relationship with the Father. I have to be careful of the words I choose to speak into others lives. To live a life in Christ, takes discipline. If we are suppose to be disciples of God's Word, that means we are to be disciplined and only through God's grace can we become disciplined.

> *Likewise, I want women to adorn themselves with proper clothing, modestly and discreetly, not with braided hair and gold or pearls or costly garments, but rather by means of good works, as is proper for women making a claim of godliness.*
> —1Timothy 2:9, 10 (NAS)

> *Women must likewise be dignified, not malicious gossips, but temperate, faithful in all things.*
> —1Timothy 3: 11(NAS)

> *Your adornment must not be merely external-braiding the hair, and wearing gold jewelry, or putting on dresses; but let it be the hidden person of the heart, with the imperishable quality of a gentle and quiet spirit, which is precious in the sight of God.*
> —1Peter 3:3,4 (NAS)

I need to take the limits off of God. I need to take off the limits of what He can do for me in my mind. This is a problem when you live a life of limits. Take the limits off! I have to take the limits off in order to get anywhere or to accomplish things in my life. To receive what God desires for me to have and be blessed with. The limits are bondage. Here is a simple example of limits.

I was exercising and trying to eat right to lose weight and everyone around me began to recognize it. One of my daughters told me that she wanted to start exercising and eating better, which is great. The following day she went walking with me. I told her to do her best, if she cannot keep up with me it is okay.

She asked me where we were going. I told her not to ask me where we are going. I told her to just walk with me, clear her mind and meditate on good things. I told her to take the limits off. She looked at me and said that she just wanted to know where we were walking to.

"I know what you are asking me, but I need you to take the limits off," I said.

"Okay," she said, and got quiet, not really understanding what I was telling her. But she continued to walk, trusting her mother. When we finished the walk, she was shocked that she was able to keep up with me and was shocked how far she actually walked.

"If I had told you how far we were going to walk, or where we were walking to, you would have said no way," I said. "You would have had the limits on and limited yourself. You would have immediately told me what you cannot do."

Unfortunately, many people limit their lives. This may be one of the reasons that God does not give us details of our journey because if we knew what it entailed we would say no, quit before we even get started. We would not trust in the Father, but live in doubt. I asked my daughter did she understand and she told me, yes, she did.

I told her, "From this day forward, you live in the land of no limits. Apply this to everything because you can accomplish anything you want to do. We serve a limitless God. If he has no limits and we are His children, then we need to be like the Father, living in the land of no limits. Our doubts hold us back. Why do we spend so much energy on what we cannot do, than what the possibilities can be or what the possibilities are? Take the limits off! Take the limits off! Take the limits off! Think about what I am saying. Really think about it. What area of your life are you placing limitations in? What areas of your life are you filling your mind up with doubt about what you can really do or get accomplished?

I say this to say that in order to become the woman of God I need to be, I cannot have limits. I need to be free. I need to be confident that the Father will move in my life in ways that I cannot imagine to accomplish in me to be the woman of God that he designed me to become. With no limits, I will get their faster than I would if I filled myself with doubt and disbelief, causing me to struggle and move slow, or not at all. That is what happens when we have limitations, right? We stay where we are, or never accomplish anything. Limitations are doubtful thinking. A life with no limitations is a life of faith.

Now faith is the substance of things hoped for, the evidence of things not seen.
—Hebrews 11:1(KJV)

But scripture has locked up everything under the control of sin, so that what was promised, being given through faith in Jesus Christ, might be given to those who believe.
—Galatians 3:22 (NIV)

But when you ask, you must believe and not doubt, because the one who doubts is like a wave of the sea, blown and tossed by the wind.
—James 1:6 (NIV)

Don't get jealous of the people who are successful; they have no limits; you do. They believe all things are possible through Christ. People of the world who are successful have to take limits off of themselves in order to propel their life forward. In my walk with the Lord, as I am becoming the woman of God that I need to be, I have to trust God in the good and bad times of my life. When Jesus died on the cross, he became the sacrificial lamb for us. We know longer have to put pigeons, doves, goats, or lambs on the altar to sacrifice for our sins. Jesus was the last lamb to ever be sacrificed for any sin that we could ever commit. He knew that it was no other way for us to be saved. When we accept Christ as our personal Lord and Savior, at that moment, we are out of the old life and walk into a new life.

Because we are sinners saved by grace, there will be times that we will sin and fall short of God's glory, knowingly and unknowingly at times, but thanks to God, He knew that our sinful nature would lead us to eternal damnation. As a result, He knew He needed to be the atonement for any sins that we committed in order to have a chance for eternal life. In becoming the woman of God I need to be, I will probably make mistakes along the way and when I repent, I will be forgiven, and the sin will be remembered no more.

Chapter 16

Mistakes

Over the years of me constantly looking for my dad on the streets, I too developed addictions. One addiction was as an enabler, also known as a codependent. The second addiction was the need to make sure my family members needs were met, and they were not on the streets. I was helping my family so much that my family came before my marriage. WRONG! WRONG! WRONG!

People have said that there is no manual on marriage, raising kids, and how to stay away from sin, yet in the Word of God all our answers are there. We are human, yes. We have a sinful nature, yes. Sin takes on a life of its own. Sin births more sin. We are going to make mistakes over and over again. We make mistakes for many reasons, besides it being how we learn whether something is wrong or right to do. Some of the sins we carry around with us are the sins that were passed down to us from generation to generation.

Those are the worse kind because they were passed down right to you despite of what the word of God said. I believe that some parents told their kids that a particular sin was not right, but God will understand, he knows how we are made. We must study the word of God to know how to live. The more we focus on doing the right thing, especially if we believe that the Bible is the final authority, then day by day, with God's help we will sin less and make less mistakes. We must pray to God and ask him to help us. We are supposed to be world overcomers anyway. But know this, even though we pray there is an adversary that is going to and fro, seeking whom he may devour. I pray that everyone that chooses to live for God understands that the adversary has already been defeated and God gives us the strength to conquer sin in our lives.

> *For we wrestle not against flesh and blood, but against principalities, against powers, against rulers of the darkness of this world, against spiritual wickedness in high places.*
> —**Ephesians 6:12, (KJV)**

Well, you may be wondering or asking the question, "Kim, how did you come up with all of this? What made you write this book? How did you come to realize, or come to the conclusion that when you were looking for your dad, you should have been looking to the Father?"

While I was going through all these trials and tribulations of life, I did not have a clue. We all learn from someone else's or our own mistakes. Our mistakes help us to help someone else not to make the same mistakes. The saying goes, we go through things individually, not for ourselves, but someone else. God always brings someone in your path (life) that will be involved or entering that same or similar situation. God can then use you, the individual to help others by telling your story and it saves or helps them. I have seen it over and over again. Let's not forget because we have the freedom of choice. This does not mean that the individual will take the advice from us and use it, but it is giving that person an option to chose what he or she will do with the information given.

If they do not, you just move on, then shake the dust off your feet. Some of us need an earthquake, which is what happened to me. I ask myself, why did it have to take an earthquake for me to get it? I see now that the shaking from the quake is what I needed to help me. My journey, if I could describe it, has been like God is the contractor, and I am the construction project. His angels go to work on His behalf and move according to the words I speak out of my mouth. When I stop listening and start speaking contrary to the Word, my mouth shuts down the construction. When I ask for help, the construction begins again right where it left off. I wanted my prayers answered, and they were getting answered. In the process I was losing sight of what was important. I lost myself and was trying to fix everyone else.

God answers prayers. I do not want anyone to think that their prayers are not being heard. Your prayers are heard just like mine were. Some prayers are not answered in the way we expect them to be answered. Sometimes the answer to the prayers will be NO! Other times, the answer is YES! Whether the answers of your prayer has been answered by God, no or yes, the prayer has been answered.

One Sunday, my pastor made a statement that was profound. He said, "My fear, my concern, for my flock is that most of you are one NO! away from turning from God. For those of you whom may not be familiar with the term flock, that is the church, the congregation, or the followers."

I never want to be that person my pastor is speaking of. God is good even when he says NO!! God's no could be the difference between me having peace love, prosperity, joy, grace, safety, mercy. God's favor versus no peace, hate, bitterness, depression, lack, doubt, total destruction.

John C. Maxwell_ "A man must be big enough to admit his mistakes, smart enough to profit from them, and strong enough to correct them."

James Joyce_ "Mistakes are the portals of discovery."

There are things that need to be in place first in your life before some prayers are answered. God has equipped us all with various gifts, skills, and talents, and some of those gifts, skills or talents have not been tapped into. They are lying dormant, undiscovered.

Remember God knows the plans that He has for us, plans to prosper us and give us a hope and a future. God is always talking to His children in a still small voice, and if we would only get in His presence, for Him to tell us. God gives us gifts and abilities, for a job, writing books, teaching, sometimes auxiliaries in the church, careers that will minister to others, to just be a light in a dark place, which will give Him glory.

You may have been given, visions, dreams of teaching, preaching, and mission work here in the United States, or in another part of the world for the Kingdom of God. God has plans and purposes for our lives. Many of us have had God tell us what He is going to do for us. He has directed us towards something or someone, and we believe what He has said. We receive what He has said, and then move in that direction by faith. We take the leap of faith. We say, "Okay, God. We know you are going to see this through, because this is what you said."

Some of us get real close, and some of us are able to walk by faith no matter what happens. For example, you start up a business and it folds. Some of us have been promoted on jobs and then get fired. I can go on and on, I believe you understand what I am trying to say. We are in an "I-Want-It-Now" society. We have such an advanced technology; it has become a blessing and a curse to a lot of us in more ways than one. We rush the process and step out on "self," instead of faith. We try to figure out how to get things accomplished all at once. We act as if we were given the beginning, the middle, and the ending all at the same time.

The thing is, is when it does not manifest immediately or in the time clock we set for it to happen, we get upset. We go to God and say, "What am I supposed to do now?"; "Lord I thought you said this is what I am supposed to be doing?" Or you'll say, "Lord!" I thought you said this was my husband or my wife.""Lord, why did you tell me to do this, if you were going to let it fail?" or, "Why, Lord?" You become frustrated, discouraged, and even angry. Let me just keep it real.

In the beginning, we were excited about what God was saying, on such a high, but when it went south, some of us gave up. Then there are those who do not give up. This does not mean it did not affect them, but they understood that God has His reasons, or a better plan. I heard a pastor say once, "The Holy Spirit unveils things you cannot see. The Holy Spirit unveils the things that are designed for your life. The Holy Spirit is not just power, but intelligence." The angels could simply be in war, trying to get our prayers answered like Daniel, in the book of Daniel. In the book of Daniel 10:2-7, it talks about Daniel being on a fast for three weeks, twenty-one days. Daniel sees a vision of an angel, which speaks to him, he describes the encounter.

> *Then he said, "Don't be afraid, Daniel. Since the first day you began to pray for understanding and to humble yourself before your God, your request has been heard in heaven. I have come in answer to your prayer. But for twenty-one days the spirit prince of the kingdom of Persia blocked my*

> *way. Then Michael, one of the archangels, came to help me, and I left him there with the spirit prince of the kingdom of Persia.*
>
> **—Daniel 10:12,13, (NLT)**

Then there are those individuals who will talk to God and say, "Well, Lord, you said it, so in your time, Lord." Those who say, "Lord, I do not know how you are going to do it, but I thank you that it is done," or "Lord, I trust you! I am going to trust you, Lord, even though it looks bad," or, "Lord, I leave this in your hands."

God knows His plans and purposes for us, His purposes do not change, but the way He wants the purpose fulfilled can change. God created us. We did not create Him and He knows what is best for our lives and it is far better than what we can ever imagine for ourselves. We need to trust the Word of God, which is God, per John 1:1. We must learn to live by the Word of God.

In my life, there were certain events that needed to take place before certain blessings happened for me. Certain ideas came to me, and before God gave me plans and answers, He first had to work on me in areas of my life. After that, parts of God's purpose began to manifest itself in my life. I had to heal and overcome my past wounds. I needed to get rid of some baggage that I was carrying around with me.

Chapter 17

I Was Carrying Baggage, But The Baggage Got Too Heavy

I had so many bags I was carrying until I was just stuck in one spot. The baggage was impossible to carry by myself; I needed help. You may ask, Kim, what was the baggage that you were carrying around? Here are some of the baggage I had been through:

1. Baggage of Disappointment
2. Baggage of Failure
3. Baggage as an Enabler
4. Baggage of Low Self-Esteem
5. Baggage of not Knowing my Self-Worth
6. Baggage of Passiveness
7. Baggage of Dishonesty
8. Baggage of Promiscuity

I had so much baggage, and it has taken me almost five years to heal from most of it. The baggage caused me to get myself in a mess, which led ultimately to the writing of this book. The baggage of disappointment was a result of my poor judgment of character when it came to the type of men that chose me and the men I accepted in my life. I had allowed myself to open my heart too quickly and to become an easy read. Usually, the relationship would go sour.

First, I carried the baggage of failure: Failure is a lack of performance, a lack of success. I felt like a failure. I felt that I was not being a positive role model to my children. At times, I stayed in a relationship that was going nowhere. And because of a divorce, it has caused my children to question the importance of being in a marriage and their understanding of what love means. Moreover, I had not completed college. I felt like I was unsuccessful in the business world, and my children were looking up to me. It made me feel like a failure.

Second, I had the baggage of an enabler is one that enjables another to achieve an end; especially one who enables another to persist in self-destructive behavior (such as substance abuse) by providing excuses, or by making it possible to avoid the consequences of such behavior. I constantly made excuses and tried to justify my dad's behavior, as well as a couple of other family members. I was an enabler to my Dad in his addiction.

Third, I was burdened with the baggage of low self-esteem: Self-esteem is defined as a confidence and satisfaction in oneself combined with self-respect. I was the complete opposite. Self-worth is a feeling that you are a good person who deserves to be treated with respect. I tried to *please everybody else*. I tried to take care of everyone else, and, in the meantime, *I lost myself*. I no longer considered my needs, my feelings, my goals, or my desires. This was part of me—the not knowing my self-worth.

Next, I was strapped with the baggage of passiveness. To be passive is described as someone who allows things to happen, or who accepts what other people do, or decides without trying to change anything. Passiveness was awful, because when I should have addressed certain things with people, I did not, and, thus, people were just running all over me. Everybody would call me with their difficulties, and I became the chauffeur or trash can for everyone's problems. It was taking from my rest and the time I should have had for my children and myself.

The baggage of distrust: distrust is the lack of trust or confidence: a feeling that someone or something is not honest and cannot be trusted, the lack or absence of trust. It was hard to trust people. I was running into so many dishonest people that when people were being honest with me I did not believe them.

Last, I carried the baggage of Promiscuity, Promiscuous behavior is characterized by, or involving indiscriminate mingling or association, especially having sexual relations with several partners on a casual basis. This can consist of parts, elements, or individuals of different kinds brought together without order. My promiscuity was a result of a rape. This is one of the worst crimes there is. Rape can also mean to plunder or strip something of resources. There are few words more powerful than rape, which is a horrifying crime, most often done by a man to a woman.

Chapter 18

The Trickster

This not pleasant, but here we go. I was very shy and I stuck pretty much to myself, if I did not know you. I would eventually gain more friends. I had met this senior at school. I will refer to him as the Trickster. He was in my third period class, I believe. The Trickster would try to get my attention and even went as far as finding out my name. He seemed like he was an okay guy. When the Trickster found out that I lived right around the corner from him, he would come by the house. He was very respectful and well-mannered to my parents and portrayed himself to be a great guy. He had a really nice '65 Mustang which was given to him by his father. Trickster would drive around the corner and pick me up to spend time with me. One day Trickster asked me if I would be his girlfriend.

"That's okay, but no sex," I replied.

"Okay, that is no problem." Trickster sounded sincere.

"Are you a virgin?" I asked.

"Yes, I am, and I want to stay that way until I get married," Trickster said, "Just as you should." He reassured me that I did not have to worry about him at all.

One day Trickster called me up on the phone and asked me could I come over and help his little sister with her homework because he was not feeling well. I told him okay that was no problem. When I arrived, his little sister was outside playing. His dad was about to leave for work. I noticed about 6-8 of his friends were on the side of his house, talking to him through his bedroom window.

I went inside of the house and started helping his little sister with her math homework. Twenty minutes into the work, he calls his sister to his room.

When she comes back to the front she tells me, "My brother wants you to come back there with him."

"No!" I yelled down the hallway. "I am here to help your sister and you are sick. I do not want to get sick."

I finished helping her with her homework and yelled to Trickster, "I am going to go now. I hope you feel better."

"No, come here for a minute, just a minute," he yelled back,

I hesitated. I did not feel right for some reason, but I went back to his room and stood at the door. I believe I was not comfortable especially because his Dad was not home. He was lying on his bed.

"What do you want?" I asked, standing in the door way.

"Come here and sit down on the cedar chest." He pointed to the chest at the foot of his bed. I agreed to sit there for one minute. I was nervous and as I walked in his room, I noticed some lines of white powder and a razor blade on the dresser. He crawled down to the end of the bed.

"Come up here on the bed with me."

"No, I'm leaving." I stood up.

"No, no, okay… just sit down. You do not have to get on the bed, " he said.

I finally relented and sat back down. I guess he called himself wanting to play. His sister ran back to the room, and he told her to go outside and play for a little bit, she agreed and left out.

He started grabbing me, acting like he was playing, but I told him to stop because he was hurting me. He took his hand and grabbed my wrist, pulled me on the bed. I told him to stop again. I told him he was hurting me. He didn't pay my cries any attention. He held my wrists with one hand and tore the crotch of my jeans with the other.

"No! Stop!" But he would not stop. He forced himself on me, and I was horrified. When he was done, he got up, and I ran out the house. His friends were coming from the side of the house laughing.

I ran and jumped on the bus to go to the valley where my mom stayed and my favorite cousin. When I got on the bus, I balled myself up in the seat. My jeans were ripped and blood running down my legs. Some people asked me, "Miss, are you okay?" or "What's wrong?"

I balled up tighter. "Leave me alone," I cried.

Once I got to the valley where my family lived, I had the strangest thought in my head that my mom was not going to believe me.

I walked to the corner and called my favorite cousin from the payphone. I screamed in the phone and cried, he raped me, I told him no. What am I going to do?

I remembered a lady that lived on my dad's street that told me if I needed her, I could always call her, so that is what I did, I called her. When I called her and told her, she asked where I was. I told her. I asked and begged her not to tell my dad. She asked could I get to her, or did I want her to come and get me.

I called my favorite cousin and told her that I was going to meet her. She said she is going to take me to get help. When I got to her, she gave me a hug and took me to this clinic, I could not tell you which one because I was so out of it. The nurses came in and talked to me. Then the doctor talked to me. They asked me what happened, even though my dad's friend had explained to them. I was so violated and even in the room with them, it seemed as if it was never going to end. I had to take my clothes off so they could examine me. I remember the doctor and nurse being upset. The doctor asked me what he used on me. I told them himself. He raped me.

I cannot describe to you how grotesque this was. They had to check me for diseases. They wanted me to see a counselor for help. I cannot even tell you everything she said because the more she talked, the sound of her voice just sounded muffled. The only thing I remember her saying was, "You have to talk about it. Get it out.

When I returned to school, I was so terrified, I wanted to go back home. I did not want to see him. I did not know what was happening to me, I thought I was losing my mind and before I would let that happen I began to talk, to the wrong people that is. I told my friends that I thought were my friends and asked them not to say anything, but it got out anyway. You see my friends were upset because of what happened and wanted me to get justice. I was alone. When the Trickster found out, he approached me and asked me why I was saying that he raped me.

"Because you did," I said.

"No, I did not," he said, then walked away.

Remember, I told you that we had a class together. Well, in this classroom, the teacher had the class split in half, with each half of the class facing each other. I was on the first row of the right half and he was on the second row on the left side of the class. He put up the finger to me and laughed at me. The teacher was called out of the class for a minute. In her absence, he stood up in class turned around dropped his pants and mooned me. I could not take it anymore. I got up and ran out of the classroom, crying.

The teacher was entering back in the class as I was leaving, and called me.

"Where are you going?" she asked.

I told her that I was so sorry; I could not stay in her class.

She asked me why and I told her that I was raped by my ex-boyfriend that is in her class. She asked me did I report it. I told her that no one would believe me and I left. In those days, it was not the same situation as now. Teachers did not have to report my situation. Fortunately,

I did not have to worry about him anymore the rest of the school year because he went to jail for possession of drugs.

I did, however, run into Trickster again, years later, walking down the street. He stopped me and wanted to talk, I said hello and kept walking. You see, I forgave him and moved on with my life. I had a lot of problems that developed from this horrific incident, but I wanted to go on with my life. I could not give up on life.

After that incident, I had several sexual partners, I did not know how to say no. If the guy I was dating asked, I automatically said yes, I figured, if I said yes, they would not rape me. I was so confused. I did not even know who I was becoming. I did not like sex. I had no help, really, to get me through all of this.

My friends could not understand what I was going through, nor could they relate. It did not happen to them, it happened to me. I figured in my mind maybe this was considered healing when I explained what happened to me. It did not feel like I was healing, but if the doctors said that talking about it would help me heal. Well, that must be true, they are the doctors, right? The way I was going about it was wrong. I did not follow the advice of the doctors, accurately. I was following my interpretation of what the doctor said.

I must admit that I was a victim of rape, but I was leaving behind some victims of my own. What do you mean, Kim? Well, some guys that I met really were taking interest in me, but I had no interest what so ever in them. I saw weaknesses in them and I was with them for my own sorted gain. I was targeting the less desirable. In some kind a way, I felt like I had more control and was dominant because of the weaknesses I saw in them. They wanted to try to have a relationship with me, but I was too messed up emotionally. I did not know how to explain it and they could not help me or change my way of thinking. This is why I say broken people need to seek the proper help to prevent walking around as damaged goods and creating problems in other people's lives.

Chapter 19

Can You Get Me There, Father?

There were times when I would request a departure from earth to heaven. The emotional turmoil was too much! I was not thinking about suicide. I was thinking about being with the Father for all eternity in heaven and not suffering here on earth. I would go in my room and talk to God. I would tell the Lord that I did not want to be here anymore. I would ask the Lord to come and get me and take me up to be with him in heaven. I did not want to die. I wanted the Lord to come and get me. Enoch walked with God and God took him. You can read this in, Genesis 5:21-24. Enoch did not die and also, Elijah was taken to heaven you can read in 2Kings2:9-11. These men never died and so I asked God to take me, too!

I told him that I could be there with Him and never have to worry about being hurt. I would jump up towards heaven, as if I was going to take flight. I knew that God had the power to do that, but it was not what God had in mind apparently, otherwise I would have been there a long time ago. I believe that God had work for me to do here on earth for His glory. I know I am not the only one that has felt that way.

I recently was engaged in conversation with one of my daughters, telling this story and she began to laugh. "Oh, my God, Momma!"

I use to say that too! I told her that God has work for her to do just like me and she is living proof because if I had been in heaven I would not have had she and her sisters. One of my jobs was to raise she and her sisters up in the Lord. Teaching you girls how to put God first in your lives. I needed to teach you what was the right way and wrong way of doing things and so much more.

God has work for all of us to do. In due season, the nature of that work or works will be revealed. The world has not always been kind, but God has. I have not always felt loved by those I thought loved me, but God has loved me from the beginning of time. I have not always made the best decisions, but God has forgiven me of all my sins. I have been anxious about some things, but God told me not to be. He told me to pray with thanksgiving and make my request known to Him. Many a times my heart has been heavy and yet God always comforts me. I have felt abandoned, even disconnected, but God has never left me nor forsaken me. My faith has been low at times, almost seemed like I did not have any faith, but God said that all I need is a grain of a mustard seed. When others find fault in me, God loves me just as I am. When I have lacked the things that I had need of, God was very generous and supplied my needs. When I lacked wisdom, God told me to ask for it. God is so amazing, how can we not, honor, praise, and give him glory. Can you come and get me Father, I say no more. I ask him to help me live a life that is well pleasing to Him, so on that great day when I am before Him in judgment, that he says, "Well Done, My Good And Faithful Servant!!!

Chapter 20

No Help After The Separation

Another major event that happened in my life was a divorce from my first and only marriage. Divorce is a spiritual death, a legal dissolution of a marriage by a court. It is a split, disunity, alienation, separation, and so much more. No one told me that things were about to get rough for me after my divorce. No one explained to me that the separation from my spouse, whether the relationship was good, bad or indifferent, that it was going to feel like a death. Let me even say that those who have lost a spouse due to a death suffer as well. I have not seen many churches that have a ministry strictly for the divorced or those who have lost a spouse. I believe the divorced and those who have lost a spouse need a support group to help them get through the difficult times that they are not aware of and they will be faced with.

There are so many people pointing the finger, telling you where you went wrong or that you have no grounds for the divorce, than trying to help you, much less pray for you. The devil came to kill steal and destroy, but God came that we may have life more abundantly. Where is the love to help our brother and sister in Christ get their lives back on track after a devastation of a divorce, or a loss of a spouse.

Some people are so quick to put God in a box and talk to you like God would never forgive you once you repent. I did not anticipate that I was going to be feeling lonely. The loneliness is like being in a wilderness lost by yourself and no one can hear your cry for help. It is like not knowing how to function in life; just being able to do the regular things or routines you have done for years.

When you have a spouse that you have shared intimacy with, quality time, pleasurable or not, it is a habit that now is broken. You were one, now split in two. How do you deal with your hormones? How do you deal with the anger? How do you deal with the loneliness? How do you deal with the fear of moving on, moving forward, when you have been off the dating market for ten plus years? How do you stay focused and in prayer when your flesh has taken on a mind of its own? What are you to do with yourself? Who is going to help you because you realize that your bed is empty? There is no one there to cuddle up to, and communicate with. When you think you are going to be okay sleeping in your bed all by yourself. Your mouth can be saying you're good, but your mind and flesh are in an all out war. It turns into World War III in your room and you are the casualty. You are hurt, bruised, and wounded.

Is it okay that you start putting pillows around yourself to feel as though someone is there? Does the pillow really become the substitute? No, it does not, but it is a temporary comforting, a quick fake fix. It is a rough road that has lead people down terrible roads. Some couples begin to abuse one another because of the loss. One example is when you are trying to make your ex-spouse suffer because of your loneliness. Some people have such difficulty with the newness of loneliness that they sometimes walk through the door of fornication, adultery, you name it because they are trying to fill the emptiness and loneliness inside. It is unnerving how the flesh is so strong at that point. When we try to do things alone on our own, without the help of the Father, we go about it all the wrong way.

> *For I know that nothing good dwells in me, that is, in my flesh; for the willing is present in me, but the doing of good is not. For the good that I want, I do not do, but I practice the very evil that I do not want. But if I am doing the very thing I do not want, I am no longer the one doing it, but sin which dwells in me.*
>
> —Romans 7:18-20(NAS)

> *For the mind set on the flesh is death, but the mind set on the Spirit is life and peace, because the mind set on the flesh is hostile toward God; for it does not subject itself to the law of God, for it is not able to do so.*
> —Romans 8:6,7 (NAS)

The worse part about it, you are susceptible to attaching yourself to someone new without airing out first. Marriage is not something that people should rush into. A lot of people are in love with the idea of having a wedding, all the glitter, glam, partying, dressing up, etc., not having or being in a marriage, being in a covenant relationship. When the party is over, the honeymoon is over, and everyone has gone home after celebrating you and your spouse, it is you and your spouse alone. Learning how to live together, in harmony with one another, yet as a united front. It gets real, real fast, you need to understand that marriage is not like Burger King, "Have it your way." In all your getting, please, get an understanding before entering the sanctity of marriage. Get sound marriage counseling. You may need to include relationship counseling and possibly couple therapy before the marriage counseling.

What is the resolution? What do we need to do? Well, if you are not willing as an individual to do the work prescribed by the counselor or therapist, then it is not going to work. Pride comes before destruction. The only one that can destroy you is you. The devil goes to work trying to destroy you. You cannot be successful in anything if you do not put the proper time and work into it. Anything worth having is going to take work and in some cases, you may have to fight for it. Remember that you dated your mate first before you got married and you will need to continue to date your mate after marriage, for we are always growing and forever changing. But with the use of the proper tools, you will come out on top.

> *The man said, "This is now bone of my bones, flesh of my flesh; she shall be called woman, for she was taken out of man." That is why a man leaves his father and mother and*

> *is united to his wife, and they become one flesh. Adam and his wife were both naked and felt no shame.*
> **—Genesis 2:23-25 (NIV)**

I was dealing with internal tragedies and my emotions were unstable. I had not realized that I was in unfamiliar territory. I was vulnerable and about to walk into this territory and create more of a mess for myself. Three months after the divorce, I found myself praying to God and creating a list of attributes I wanted the husband for me to have, if and when I got married again.

Chapter 21

The Forgery

I was not thinking that the enemy was listening to my prayers as well. I had a friend from my past that was supportive during this transition in my life at least I thought so. He helped me move into my new place, we went out and hung out at least four to five days a week, we talked a lot, especially about the past. Did you hear what I said? We talked about the past a lot. The conversations we had together were only from past memories.

Unfortunately, it did not dawn on me that the conversations were of past memories, he had been in the past for twenty-five years and now he is in my present. It was like, he only wanted to remember the past. Back down memory lane should have been the theme of his conversation. It is not that talking about past memories are bad, they are memories, and I have some great memories from my past. I was trying to get to know the present person. I wanted him to get to know the present me. Even though, I am not defined by my past, I was of my past.

I was still a broken person, wounded and bruised, fresh out of an eighteen-year marriage, which made me vulnerable prey. In the beginning, we were reminiscing of the good old times, but it was the subject matter of relationships, whether he was involved in or interested in. I did not pay attention to the conversation about the girls, until after the fact. It was as if I placed the information in storage and when things fell apart, it came to my remembrance. The Forgery had ulterior motives. I was on the phone recently with another friend from my past, which I will refer to as Never Moves Forward, and as we were talking, he kept saying, you remember back in the day when we use to hang out? I got annoyed with it and told him, that I am not my past. Question, did time stop for him and move forward for me? Did he get caught in a twilight zone or something?

"I have changed, why are you not trying to get to know the person, that I have become now?" I asked, "I am nowhere like the Kim, you once knew, I have grown up and healed from my past." These are what I call The Rearview Mirror Conversations. Never Moves Forward said, "now there you go".

"I am not trying to get to know someone new. I rather be with someone from my past that I know and she knows me."

"Why can't you give a brother a chance?"

"It takes too much time to try to get to know someone new."

"I don't have time for that."

"Never Moves Forward, why can't you learn how to be a friend?"

"Relationships come and go."

"When they are over, they are over, but real friends will be there always."

"Learn how to be my friend," I said.

"Whatever," he said.

" I know you"

I said, "No you do not know me."

"We had not been around each other in about twenty years and I do not know you, nor do you know me. I only know the person before you got married. We both got married and a lot of changes have taken place in our lives. In the process, we were getting older and we started to think differently."

"Whatever, I know you," he said.

Needless to say, that conversation ended.

You may be wondering, what am I implying when I say rearview mirror conversations? I will explain. Automobiles have a way for you to look behind you when you are driving, so that you can back up the vehicle; see if someone is driving too close to you, to back the vehicle up; or to know if someone is following you. It is called a rearview mirror.

The rearview mirror is a very small mirror usually affixed to the the front windshield. You can adjust the height and viewing angle for any driver. You can only take glances; so in essence, in looking through the rearview mirror you can miss things. The rearview mirror is augmented by one or more side view mirrors.

Recently, rearview video cameras have been built into many of the new model cars. This was partially in response to the rear view mirrors inability to show the road directly behind the automobile. It is said that as many as fifty small children are killed by SUV's every year in the United States because the driver cannot see them in the rearview mirrors. The new technology of the cameras in these new model vehicles are being attached to the rear bumper. There is still a small screen that you look at. The screen is built in the dashboard that shows you what is in the back of the vehicle. You still have to look forward, in front of you at a screen to see what is behind you. The conversations with, the Forgery, as well as Never Moves Forward, we're not going forward, they were dead.

The conversations with, the Forgery, kept me in the past. It takes more effort to look back then to look forward. If you look back too long, you cannot see what is in front of you, and that can cause a collision with the vehicle that is in front of you. You cannot get to your future, what God has in stored for you in this present life. Trust me, I can go on and on by looking backwards. The front view, is wide open out of the windshield in the front of the automobile. Life has many possibilities when you look through that wide-open view, right in front of you. I will refer to this character as, The Forgery. The enemy shined the light on the Forgery and had me thinking, 'Man the Forgery had pretty much all of the characteristics I had on my list. The enemy had me believing I knew the Forgery, when I actually did not know the Forgery. The Forgery was familiar to me.

Because the Forgery was familiar to me, I allowed that familiar spirit to get up close and personal with me. Allowing a familiar spirit in is not always good. At least, it was not good for me with the Forgery. First, I was not ready to deal with a new relationship. Two, the timing was off. Three,

I did not seek God to ask if the Forgery was not the man for me, nor did I wait for the answer. Four, it was not of God, nor blessed by God, it had no foundation. Here I am out of one frying pan and into another. My prayer life that I had, had stopped completely. Studying the Word of God went out of the window and anything else that was in God's Will for my life was pushed away. I picked up new habits, like drinking excessively, engaged in inappropriate activities, lying, the use of profanity, no need to go any further. You have an idea where I am going with this?

I was getting comfortable in the sin. I went from having a list of what I wanted in a husband to a disposition of not ever getting married again. I figured it out, at least, I thought I had it all figured out. I planned to stay in this relationship with my old friend and be content. I was choosing to settle, it felt better to settle, not to believe for better. I was just living the lie. I want you to understand that this was all the flesh. I really did say this to myself. I liked the way the relationship was going and I had decided that I would continue with this relationship with the Forgery. My attitude was that I was cool just the way things were. Man, I just believed the lie, and I was lying to myself.

I told myself that I would just have this relationship and be cool, really I did! I said, "I like the way this relationship is between Forgery and me. The Forgery knows me. We go way back to high school." I know now that in no way had this been a good situation for me. The relationship was dissolved over a picture. The picture situation was a way out of the relationship for the Forgery, an excuse out, to make a long story short. This was confusing because I did not understand why this relationship was being destroyed, when it was so perfect. Perfect, really? Everything felt right to my flesh because I got comfortable in it. In no way, was I thinking clearly.

I was trying to rationalize this in my head. I said, "I am not asking the Forgery to marry me. I am not trying to get married; I just got out of a marriage and had not planned on getting married in the near future. I was not asking for a commitment. I just wanted things to stay the way they were." *Crazy! Crazy! Crazy!* Was that deception from me or the devil?

The deceptive spirit wanted me to believe that and because I had been feeding my flesh and not my spirit man, I fell for that lie hook, line, and sinker. God said that the body is not for immorality, but for the lord, and the Lord is for the body, it states in 1Corinthians 6:13 (NAS), the last sentence in that verse. I heard a pastor once say, "Wherever Satan sets up shop, it is going to be garbage." I know that God knew what was best. *Thank you, Lord!* He was not going to give up on His child; *Me!* He was going to close this door, shut this destructive situation down.

> *Therefore, dear brothers and sisters, you have no obligation to do what your sinful nature urges you to do. For if you live by its dictates, you will die. But if through the power of the Spirit you put to death the deeds of your sinful nature, you will live. For all who are led by the Spirit of God are children of God. So, you have not received a spirit that makes you fearful slaves, instead, you received God's Spirit when he adopted you as his own children.*
> —**Romans 8:12-15, (NLT)**

When God delivers us out of certain situations and circumstances, he does not tell us how he is going to do it. In my life, when God moved, it caused me to be broken more than the brokenness I was feeling at the time. I felt the brokenness from what he was removing out of my life, or what he was taking away from me. All breakups are not necessary or mandatory, but in my case, in order to live a life that was pleasing to the Father every move he made was mandatory and necessary. I walked into the relationship broken, I ultimately suffered more brokenness because I was trying my best to hold onto the circumstances that was causing me to broken, and the Father came right on in and had to break me out from the brokenness I was in. Everything that was leading me in a downward path had to be broken off of me in order for me to get better, do better, and live better. The Father knows what we need and what we do not need. We just need to trust him and he will work everything out for our good.

The Forgery immediately got involved into another relationship.

Eight months later, the Forgery moved out of state and got married. I found out about the marriage on social media. I sent him a message of congratulations, wished him well, and just deleted him off my social media. The marriage, unfortunately, did not last more than 5months. I know you are asking, well, how did you find out months later when you said you deleted him? We had mutual friends and one of the friends close to me who knew about the Forgery and I, our relationship informed me. She was upset about the circumstances around this relationship and was interested to see just how far this marriage of his was going to go. She thought he was kind of unstable, anyway. She was also a mutual friend of his wife, who also went to highschool with us. It's a small world. Immediately, after the relationship with the Forgery was over, I was angry and bitter at first, that this life, I had grown accustomed to with the Forgery, was over.

Over those next eight months, while he had gone on with his new life, I found myself praying for the Forgery. I wanted things to go well for him. I forgave the Forgery and asked God to forgive me. You see what happens when God breaks us away from ungodly situations and circumstances? I had to forgive myself, so that I could move forward as well. I needed healing, but I prayed that the Forgery would be successful. In forgiving the Forgery, I became free, I was not hanging on and giving him power over my emotions, especially with him going on with his life. Too many people hold onto what someone has done to them and carrying that anger, resentment, and bitterness. You are miserable and the one that hurt you is living their life. They are no longer thinking about you, but every other word or statement that comes out of your mouth is about how that individual hurt you or how you hate that person because what they supposedly did to you. Stop! Stop! Stop giving them that power, you are giving them power and they do not know they have power over you. Free yourself, allow God to free you and move forward please!

> Till I come, devote yourself to [public and private] reading, to exhortation (preaching and personal appeals), and to teaching and instilling doctrine. Do not neglect

the gift which is in you, [that special inward endowment] which was directly imparted to you [by the Holy Spirit] by prophetic utterance when the elders laid hands upon you [at your ordination]. Practice and cultivate and meditate upon these duties; throw yourself wholly into them [as your ministry], so that your progress may be evident to everybody. Look well to yourself [to your own personality] and to [your] teaching; persevere in these things [hold to them], for by so doing you will save both yourself and those who hear you.
> —1 Timothy 4:13-16, (AMP)

I prayed for healing of the Forgery's mind, body, and soul. I prayed that he would have joy, peace, patience, trust, and forgiveness. Where did that come from? This was the beginning of my freedom and I was not aware of it.

> *But I tell you, Love your enemies and pray for those who persecute you. To show that you are the children of the Father Who is in heaven; for He makes the sun rise on the wicked and on the good, and makes the rain fall upon the upright and the wrong doers[alike].*
> — **Matthew 5:44,45, (AMP)**

> *If your enemy is hungry, give him bread to eat; and if he is thirsty, give him water to drink. For in doing so, you will heap coals of fire upon your head, and the Lord will reward you.*
> — **Proverbs 25:21 (AMP)**

> *Invoke blessings upon and pray for the happiness of those who curse you, implore God's blessing (favor) upon those who abuse you [who revile, reproach, disparage, and highhandedly misuse you].*

—**Luke 6:28 (AMP)**

God did not want me to remain in the deception. It was a battle to get the relationship out of my spirit. The good thing is that this situation started my prayer life back up. The first prayer I prayed was for the Forgery, and then I prayed to the Lord to heal me of this soul tie relationship. I asked God to clear up, erase the blood tie that connected me to the Forgery and every other intimate relationship from my past.

Chapter 22

Soul Ties Have To Go Now

I needed and wanted to be delivered from all of the souls I was tied to. In the book of 1 Corinthians, Paul is talking to the Church of God at Corinth. He says to the church in 1 Corinthians,6: 15-18.

Do you not know that your bodies are members of Christ? Shall I then take away the members of Christ and make them members of a prostitute? May it never be! Or do you not know that the one who joins himself to a prostitute is one body with her? For He says, "THE TWO SHALL BECOME ONE FLESH."

Satan is an accuser of the brethren. He will bring up dormant relationships that are not always healthy or good for you to purse. When I say relationships, it means all types of relationships. When these relationships come in contact with you, they bring you suddenly back in acquaintance with a negative past. Doors like these sometimes have to be completely shut.

> *Rescue me, O my God, out of the hand of the wicked, out of the grasp of the unrighteous and ruthless man.*
> **—Psalms 71:4, (AMP)**

> *Unto you do I cry, O Lord my Rock, be not deaf and silent to me, lest, if you be silent to me, I become like those going down to the pit [the grave]. Hear the voice of my supplication as I cry to You for help, as I lift up my hands toward Your innermost sanctuary(the Holy of Holies).*
> **—Psalm 28:1, 2, (AMP)**

> *Do not withhold your mercy from me, Lord; may love and faithfulness always protect me. For troubles without number surround me; my sins have overtaken me, and I cannot see. The are more than the hairs of my head, and my heart fill within me. Be pleased to save me, Lord; come quickly, Lord, to help.*
>
> —**Psalm 40:11-13(NIV)**

I have prayed and asked God to forgive me and heal me from all soul ties that I have ever had in my life. I asked God to forgive me and heal me of everything ungodly, everything that has been against His will and purpose for my life, that was tied up in all my past relationships. I did not want to be bound by my past. I prayed that God would make me new and fresh. When God blesses me to remarry, I want to be a fresh and new person, not just for myself sake, but for the sake of my future husband. My future husband does not need, nor do I want him to have to deal with unnecessary baggage and connections from my past. I believe God has answered my prayers and has healed me of all soul ties and I now feel new and fresh.

This is some of my prayers that I prayed:

> *Lord, I give my life to you and everything concerning me. Lord, direct the path of my life. Help me, Lord, to stay mindful of you, especially when I am going through trials and tribulations. Lord, remove all of those around me that mean me ill will, harm, and that would try to do all manner of evil towards me and to me. Lord, keep me safe and out of harm's way in every area in my life. Lord, I apologize for leaving and forsaking you at times in my life, thinking I could handle my life alone. Lord, help me to stay focused on what is right to say and do. Lord, give me an ear to hear and receive the Word of God, eyes to see, what you want*

me to see, and a mouth that speaks the Word of God when you direct me to speak. For I know at that moment, it will be you speaking through me because you are the Word of God. Lord, help me to abide in you. Lord, keep me in your hands. I thank you that I am righteous through you. I thank you, Lord, that I am an overcomer. I thank you that I am victorious through you. I thank you, Lord, for making me a new creation, I am the head and not the tail. I am above and not beneath because of you, Lord. Lord, less of me and more of you. Amen.

Chapter 23

God Sent Me Help!

The Lord sent someone to help me unpack my baggage. He sent someone to help me start the healing process that needed to happen in my life, in order for me to move forward. The baggage I was carrying around, I had been carrying ever since my father went to live out in the streets. The baggage was so heavy, it was starting to rip at the seams. The handle of the baggage was broken, but I kept dragging it around with me. Tired and exhausted, when I released it to God and asked Him to take over, God began to help me. God cannot do anything, unless we call on Him, ask Him. God sent a man, as a vessel, to help me and I will refer to him as *the Listener* in the book. The Listener looked like an ordinary man at the time when I met him. He was a working, single man. He was living alone; his children are grown and he had a relationship with God.

I call the Listener an ordinary man, not as a description of his features, but because he is a man that is far from perfect. He is a man that makes mistakes like anybody else. He hurts, he struggles, he has good and bad days. Once the Listener and I started communicating on the phone, we would talk for hours and would not realize how late it was. We were so engulfed in conversation, we would talk about all sorts of things, no shortage in conversation when we got on the phone. I felt so free to open up with him, it was exciting. The time would go by so fast and sometimes he would have to be at work a couple of hours before we got off the phone. There was a time when he actually told me that he had to get off the phone so he could get ready for work and I remember apologizing.

The Listener said, "That's okay. I will be fine."

I believe the only reason I knew that time, because if his alarm had not gone off he would have been late to work. Long conversations over several weeks, going through the getting to know each other stage.

During that time of getting to know each other, I took a chance and decided to tell the Listener some very personal things that happened to me in certain stages of my life. Why? Why was I so comfortable with him that I could tell him these personal things about me? I cannot explain it, but somehow I felt as if I could be transparent with the Listener. I was in no way fearful about telling my story. I was not even concerned how he would take it. I had nothing to lose. I just felt like I could express myself freely and in doing that, the Listener never looked at me different. He did not look at me through judgmental eyes. I know as Christians, we are to judge ourselves and judge sin, not judge others.

> *Don't pick on people, jump on their failures, criticize their faults, unless, of course, you want the same treatment. That critical spirit has a way of boomeranging. It's easy to see a smudge on your neighbor's face and be oblivious to the ugly sneer on your own. Do you have the nerve to say, "Let me wash your face for you," when your own face is distorted by contempt?" It's this whole traveling road-show mentality all over again, playing a holier-than-thou part instead of just living your part. Wipe that ugly sneer off your face, and you might be fit to offer a washcloth to your neighbor.*
> —Matthew 7:1, 2, (MSG)

One night, after talking the Listener, he asked me if I had gotten everything off my chest. I thought about it for a couple of seconds and said, "Yes. Yes, I really did."

He asked me how did I feel.

I began with, "I feel good, I feel like a lot of weights have fallen off me, like I shredded some pounds."

"That's because you got everything out," the Listener said. "Someone finally listened to you. No one was listening to you. You got a chance to empty it all out and now you don't have to talk about it anymore."

"You know, you are right!" I agreed.

He continued, "That is why I listened and did not interrupt you when you were talking. I realized through our conversations, you were crying out for someone to listen to you, so I did just that. I knew you needed to get it all out."

I was so amazed. That was the beginning. The healing process from my past, so I could start moving towards a better me, a new future of a journey into God's purpose for me. Our lives are pre planned in advance before we arrive here. We are masterpieces completed in the spirit realm. The blueprints were already drawn up for each one of us in the spirit realm.

> *I know the thoughts and plans I have for you," says the Lord, "thoughts and plans for welfare and peace and not for evil, to give you hope in your final outcome." Then you will come and pray to Me, and I will hear and heed you. Then you will seek Me, inquire for, and inquire Me [as a vital necessity] and find Me when you search for Me with all your heart.*
> —**Jeremiah 29:11-14, (AMP)**

> *"For I know the plans I have for you," says the Lord. "They are plans for good and not for disaster, to give you a future and a hope." In those days when you pray, I will listen. If you look for Me wholeheartedly, you will find Me. "I will be found by you," says the Lord.*
> —**Jeremiah 29:11-14, (NLT)**

God has plans and purposes for our lives. God has the directions in the way the plan is to be fulfilled. The way we go about walking in our purpose, which is through Him. God told us in His Word, to seek first the Kingdom of God and His righteousness.

> *But seek ye first the kingdom of God, and his righteousness, all these things shall be added unto you. Take, therefore, no thought for the morrow; for the morrow shall take thought for the things of itself. Sufficient unto the day is the evil thereof.*
>
> —**Matthew 6:33, 34, (KJV)**

I have to admit that at one point, as I was telling the Listener about myself, I would think that he was not listening. He never interrupted me unnecessarily. He would be silent. I was thinking, *he is not listening to a word I am saying. He is probably playing games on his phone, on his computer reading something else other than listening.*

At times, some of us, when we think someone is not listening, we assume they are not. We'll say, "You're not listening to me."

I thought, *This is too good to be true, that he was really listening.* The Listener would not say I am listening, he would just begin to repeat what I said. He must have had a recorder and was taping me. He was that good at this, I remember thinking to myself.

The Listener turned out to be a true Listener. My mother told me after I got a divorce, that she would be with me every step of the way in my healing process because she was going to be learning from this situation, too. I have been blessed with the most amazing mother. I remember about a year after this statement, I got injured on my job. I was trying to figure out how I was going to be able to pay my rent and bills. Should I move to Greensboro, North Carolina, where she lives? If I did that, how was I going to get to the doctors here?

That was not going to work. While talking to my mother on the phone about what happened, my mother repeated what she said before, "I will be with you every step of the way in your healing process because I will be learning from the situation."

At the time, my mother made this statement, she also told me that God told her to stay out of the stores. She said that she was obedient and because she was obedient, she was in a position to help me. Look how God orchestrates things. My wonderful, wonderful mother. I am so thankful to God for the mother He gave me and her obedience to Him.

"Kim, you need to air out. Air out to give yourself time to heal from the marriage," Mother encouraged.

She later explained that when I give myself time to heal, I can reflect on what I learned from the relationship. She explained that to move into a new relationship and not being over the former relationship is hazardous. It is unhealthy. Airing out would be the best thing for me right now.

What ended up happening was, I had my mom on one side of me by phone, and the Listener on the other side, as my two main supporters: holding me up. Believe me, I am grateful for the support because I had been off work for three years, and God has blessed my mother's finances to help me from being homeless. There are a lot of people homeless, fighting a work injury case and I have been asked by many how have I made it. My response to them, God blessed me with a loving and giving mother and blessed her finances to help me. It is a miracle. God has made a way out of no way. He is Jehovah Jireh, my provider. My mother wrote me a letter when I was about 14 years old, when I was living back east with my grandparents at that time.

She wrote, *"Everything happens for a reason. Look for the positive side in everything. When you want to cry, smile instead. When people try to crush you, laugh at them inside yourself. People only knock you when you have traits they would like to have. Ninety percent of the time, they are inferior and insecure and try to put their guilt-trip on you. Remember, people can only do to you, what you allow them to do."* I believe everything happens for a reason, but I have to tell you the truth, when I cried. I cried, I did not smile, but I smile now, after I cry.

Majority of the time it was the Listener who had more access to me physically because my mother lived three thousand miles away, even though she and I talked, pretty much, everyday. The Listener was only driving distance from me. This is how I received my support or positive reinforcement. Fragile I was, God was working on me. He was gathering up the fragments in my life. In John 6, Jesus fed about five thousand men and had leftovers.

> *When they had all had enough to eat, he said to his disciples, "Gather the pieces that are left over. Let nothing be wasted.*
> — **John 6:12, (NIV)**

    I was in pieces, but God was saying, let nothing be wasted. The pieces of my life that were broken, were not for me. The pieces were for someone else that I was going to be a testimony to. Whomever God needs me to be a testimony to.

> Your eyes saw my unformed body; all the days ordained for me were written in your book before one of them came to be. How precious to me are your thoughts, God! How vast is the sum of them!
> —**Psalm 139:16, 17, (NIV)**

> *He who was seated on the throne said, "I am making everything new! Then he said, "Write this down, for these words are trustworthy and true." He said to me; "It is done. I am alpha and omega, the Beginning and the End. To the thirsty I will give water without cost from the spring of the water of life.*
> —**Revelation 21:5, 6, (NIV)**

Chapter 24

The Listener

God was beginning a new work in me. He was turning my life around. Life opened up anew for me after meeting the character I referred to as the Listener. I know a few of you may be curious as to how did I meet the Listener? He and I were traveling in the same direction temporarily one day. The Listener was a bus driver and one day I was heading over to my dad's house to borrow his vehicle to run some errands. I walked to the bus stop to wait for the bus. The bus pulls up, I get on the bus and try to put my money in the machine. At the same time, he is trying to block me from doing so. The Listener says you ride for free today. You would have thought I would have gone to sit down, but my mind was on other things. I try to put the money in again, he says it is broken. I was not listening, so he put his hand over the machine and said it is broken, but if you want to pay okay.

If you have ever ridden on a city bus, you will see a box behind the driver. I was standing in front of the box close to the driver because I was going to be getting off soon. My dad only lived ten minutes by car away from me. The conversation started with a warm hello from the Listener. I responded back with a hello.

I just ended the relationship with the Forgery. I was on the defense, and I had a very unpleasant attitude. Remember, God was working on me even though it did not feel like it. I was standing next to him, and he seemed to be persistent to communicate with me. I do not know why. When I look back, all I can say is Jesus knew why He had him communicating with me.

In the beginning of the conversation, I was awful. I was snappy. The Listener did not offend me, he was not rude to me, he was not snapping back, and he kept a smile on his face and a very positive attitude. He was polite, respectful and kind with his words. I was fresh out of a relationship that was not healthy. I was doing everything that was out of character for me, everything that fed my flesh and I was upset that it was over.

The Listener asked, "What do you do for a living? Do you work, go to school?"

Sarcasm was terrible from me, I said, " I work a full-time job and I go to school full- time," I said.

If it had been me, I would have said nothing to me. I would have probably been saying this heifer is crazy! I would have left me alone. This was not the normal. This was clearly God's plan because who would be crazy enough to continue talking to me. It could have been that God revealed something to him about me when he saw me or started talking to me. Truth is I have no clue why he continued talking to me, but I am thankful that he did. Funny thing is, before I knew it during the conversation, I had calmed down, started enjoying the conversation, and he put a smile on my face. Before I got off the bus one of my ringtones was playing.

The ringtone I had for my dad when he called and the Listener said, "You seem like a very nice lady, why don't you take down my phone number and give me a call."

"I do not have a pen and paper," I said.

The Listener said, with a little sarcasm in his voice, he said, "You have a phone, so go ahead and put my number in your phone."

I smiled and chuckled, and said, "Okay."

Music is supposed to sooth the savage beast, but the positive attitude and pleasant spirit of the Listener calmed me down, so I had a reasonable conversation and left his presence with a positive attitude. Like I explained earlier in the book, the Listener was the one that God sent to help me unpack my baggage. I had been on a trip far too long, if you know what I mean.

This is the same man I told you that I would talk to for hours. The one that allowed me to express myself. He listened to me tell him about my life, everything I had gone through from a child and all the way up to the point of me meeting him. Through weeks and months of conversation, I emptied my tank of past brokenness. Can I tell you something? This was actually the second time I had met the Listener. I know you are probably saying to yourself, what? Yes, It was the second time in my life, I had met him. It was not revealed to me until one day he and I were on the phone talking about names. The Holy Spirit said you met him before. It was resonating all through me. I was trying to figure out how while he was talking to me. I had to say something to him, I could not hold my tongue, if God said it to me, it had to be true.

"Listener?" I called out to him.

"Yes," he responded.

"I have met you before," I assured him.

"No you have not," he tried to reassure me.

"Yes, I have," I said confidently.

"Sure, we didn't," he said. "No, you have not because, I do not have a common name."

"I know you do not have a common name, but I have, I just have to figure out where, " I said matter-of-factly.

I know this man at this point thought I was crazy. I simply could not shake the feeling, so the conversation was taking a different turn because of a name. I began to try to think of every place, I could have possibly met him. He was so adamant that he had not met me. He was probably going through the rolodex of his mind, his little black book, cell phone contacts, and social media accounts to check. Can you imagine? I started asking several questions. I said, "What church do you attend? Have you ever been to my job location? What school did your kids attend? Have you ever gone roller skating before at World On Wheels? Skate Depot? Reseda Skating rink? Did your kids run for any track clubs? How about bowling?" There was a pause on the phone. I may have hit the jackpot.

"I bowl," he said. "That's it right there—bowling," He continued, "I bowl, but I have not met you before."

I said, "Okay. Did you bowl, in Hollywood?"

He said, "I have bowled all over."

I asked him did he bowl leisurely or on a league after naming off different bowling alleys. He named about two or three bowling alleys that he was part of a league for. When he said the last name, it was revealed to me. I told the Listener that he met me at Cal Bowl! He did not believe me so I had to rewind the tape per se. I told the Listener that when I met him I was married, and my ex-husband at the time was bowling in the same league as he was. I told him that he knew my ex-husband; one of my ex-husbands brothers that bowled; his brothers best friend, and he too was married. That got the Listeners attention. He could only agree, but was not clear on how we met, but God was, and he revealed that. Do you hear me? I told him that one league night I was at the bowling alley, with my ex-husband and my four little girls.

I recanted the following story to him: we were there to watch my ex-husband bowl. I went to get my kids something to eat and while they were eating, I walked over to the middle of the bowling alley where people stand and watch. I went to speak to my brother-in-law at the time and his friend while standing against the wall. The Listener walked from the lanes up top to where we were standing, and he engaged in a conversation with my brother-in-law. He looked to his right where I was standing and said hello and introduced himself to me. I said hello and told him my name. He then asked me how I was doing and I said fine before returning to his lane to bowl. I stood there a few minutes, and went back to where my kids were. The Listener began to think real hard. Finally, he remembered.

He said, "Yes, you have four little girls."

I confirmed "Yes, I would sit there and watch. Sometimes, I did not go to the bowling alley, I would stay home…You also, bowled against my ex-husband because after the league bowl, sometimes some of the guys would have a little side bet, bowling against one another. Somebody always felt they were the better bowler, I guess it was a man thing."

He then asked, "Who was your husband?"

I replied, "The one with the wicked ball. The one that could bowl with his left hand, right hand, and between his legs. His ball was called wicked because his ball would look like it was going to the gutter and then hit right in the pocket."

The Listener began to recall, "I remember now. You did meet me before. I was married back then."

I know from this experience for sure that the Holy Spirit will bring things to your remembrance, at least, what needs to be remembered. One day at the end of a conversation, the Listener told me that I needed to air out. I was saying to myself, here we go again with this air out stuff. I have heard this from my mother now you? What's really going on? The Listener continued and said that I need to allow myself time to heal. To come to know myself, who I am, and what it is that I want to do with my life. He also told me that I did not need to be in an intimate relationship with anyone at all right now. The Listener recognized that I was broken into different pieces, which made me vulnerable as well. The Listener did not want to take advantage of me, even though he could have. He wanted to help me. I had to start airing out, and in order for that to happen, the Listener put distance between us.

He told me that I needed to read the Word of God and pray. Once the Listener said that to me, I got quiet, emotions of abandonment were rising up in me. Insecurities were rising. The Listener was the first man that saw me. The Listener saw right through me. He understood me; he got me. I could be myself with him for the first time in my life. All my fears went out the window. For the Listener to say that I needed to air out, my heart dropped and so did my self-esteem. I was trying to take all this in at once, but it was a hard pill to swallow. The Listener explained to me that he did not want to be a rebound. He said, "You must allow yourself to heal and, in the meantime, I will be here, but in the background. God has placed me in your life to help you, so that's what I am going to do."

THE LISTENER STAYED IN THE BACKGROUND

You might be asking the question, did the Listener really stay in the background? You might be even asking, what did the Listener mean by staying in the background? What did he do while he was in the background? The first thing you need to understand is that this was very difficult for me because I was not use to this. I had never been out of a relationship in my life. It was one relationship to another. I have never aired out from any relationship. You cannot have a healthy relationship with a wounded person.

Too many of us feel like we can get into a relationship and make somebody better, by trying to be the opposite experience of what they have been through. For example, I know a man that met this lady that had suffered severe abuse at the hand of a couple of men that she was in relationship with. They physically and verbally abused her and this man felt that if he showed her how a man was suppose to treat her that this would help her. She would learn to trust men, well, at least him. It worked against him because she took his kindness for weakness and winded up verbally abusing him. Everyone could see how it was unhealthy, he would try to find all of the positive things that she had done and focused on those things in hopes that she would change.

The man made so many excuses for her that he became a victim of verbal abuse and before it was over physical abuse. Abused individuals, nine times out of ten, abuse others. They need to get help from qualified professionals that are educated in that field, that know how to help them heal from those wounds. We should never take on more than we can handle. Lord, help us not to make decisions based on a person's physical attributes, professional career, or financial status. If they are wounded inside, they are wounded. Learn to get to know the person and give yourself time to learn as much as you can about a person: because some of us hide behind our positive attributes, whatever they might be.

Have you ever tried to talk to a person and every time you turn around there's a problem? After a while, that individual is going to get on your nerves. It is mentally draining to hear negativity all the time. If you are involved in a relationship with that type of person, you will eventually exit that person's life and tell them they need help. Back to the point. I needed to air out. The Listener stayed in the background as a friend. Possible outcome, I would heal and become a stronger and better me. My focus needed to be God first. With healing would come clear decision making on what I wanted and knowing what I needed in my life. This was no easy road for me. I had to learn many things.

Believe me, there was chemistry between the Listener and myself. We liked each other a lot, but he did not want to be a rebound, or a second thought. He even made mention that it was possible that after I healed, I may not be interested in him. I may not have the desire to be in a committed relationship with him at all. But, when I make my decision whether I wanted to be with him or not, that I would be making the decision from a healed and clear mind, not a decision made from brokenness. I am grateful to God for the Listener respecting me and caring enough about me to see me healed. Taking a chance knowing that even though he liked me, in the end, I may see him differently. I thank God, the Listener was praying for me because I needed prayer all the time. The distance put between us allowed me the time to reflect on conversations we had about my children, self esteem, patience, letting go and letting God, trusting God, trusting myself, building confidence, respecting myself, others, and so much more; helped me tremendously.

I would not have been able to do this if the Listener was around me 24/7. The focus would have been on a relationship because I would have been substituting for what I had lost prior. I would have been catering to him and his needs, while continually losing more and more of myself. Ultimately, it would have been a disaster waiting to happen because I would have not grown or healed. *The distance helped me face myself.* It forced me to be alone with myself to find out who I was. To learn to love myself. How can I love anyone with the love they need and I do not even love myself? I thank God that the Listener always pointed me in the right direction, which was to God. He would say to focus on God. Remembering often, how I was grateful for help and I would tell the Listener thank you for his help, but he would say not to thank him, thank God. A four-year process it has been for me.

Chapter 25

Ms. Fix-a-Problem

In the start of this book, I told you about my dad, so you can see or imagine some of the underlying issues. I had a spirit of fear. Fear of other family members possibly being in the streets. No, my entire family was not on drugs, but lack of money for a bill, rent, food, regular necessities, lack of a vehicle and needing to get around, it was Kim to the rescue. All of this was wearin me down, but I did it anyway. I did it so long I became an enabler to grown folks that were perfectly capable of taking care of themselves. I took on a roll of being a parent to them. I was Ms. Fix-A-Problem. Every time something went wrong in the family, it was Ms. Fix-A-Problem to the rescue. This was what I call a family addiction.

I had to apologize to my children. I was hurting my children. I was taking away from them and giving to other family members. I was building up hurts and frustrations in my children. They were angry and resented those who I was helping. They were wondering why was I helping these grown people with their problems and I had four girls to raise that had needs. They wondered why were they calling and asking their mother for help, they could not figure things out on their own? This addiction was destroying the bond I had with my girls. I loved my girls, but the addiction was blinding me to the reality that was happening around me.

When I stopped trying to fix everyone else's problems, I would start praying to God about it, except, in my mind that I needed to learn the word NO. With time, the word NO became my best friend. These adults are responsible for their own lives, just like I was responsible of mine, that took away an enormous amount of stress off me. Now I say, the word No with confidence and with no regrets. I say to myself, let Jesus fix it. Jesus can fix any problem. He is the ultimate problem-solver. I began trusting God and when I need to face family issues it was not so bad. It was not for me to carry family burdens. We are suppose to cast our cares on the Lord, knowing that He cares for us. I was not alone, I had Jesus.

If it does not concern Kim, I am not in it. I like the saying, "Not my circus, not my monkeys." I do not own or run a circus, nor do I have monkeys. In essence, none of my business. We all have a year to work on this. Six months to mind our own business, and six months to leave everybody else's business alone. The Listener helped me come to the realization that I needed to allow my children to grow up. I had sheltered my children for so long that I was crippling them. I was crippling them by not allowing them to figure things out for themselves. I was not allowing my children to make mistakes so they could learn from them.

It was not that my kids were slow or incapable of learning. My children were well equipped, but the question was, when were they going to get the opportunity to use what they had been taught? How was I going to know if they had retained what they had been taught or if they were going to use their training at all? If I was going to continue to run to the rescue to tell them what and how to do everything…why should they have to think at all for themselves? Doing this was setting them up for failure. I am so glad I backed up. My children are doing just fine.

Chapter 26

Selfishness and Impatience

Being self-centered, selfish, was an issue for me. Only thinking of myself and what benefitted me. While on this journey, I found out that in the process of being healed and delivered from my old ways of doing things, it was not going to be instantaneously. There are multiple layers within that area that need to fall off. It is like shaving/scraping the scales off a fish that you caught. This is only one of the processes of preparing the fish before cooking it. In other words this process of elimination of the old you is preparing you for what God has in mind and has designed for your life. God was chiseling at me. I am not a completed work by the Father, yet while he is still removing all of the gook off me. I must continue to trust him. As the Father chisels at me, more and more of his beauty that is within me will come out. The reality of this came to me when the Listener was talking to me one evening on the phone. The Listener told me that God had been dealing with him. I was trying to find out what was going on his life. I wanted the Listener to open up to me. I was used to opening up to him. I told him that I wanted to start spending time together. I wanted to go out more. The Listener was dealing with an ill mother who he loved dearly. He had a job a with fluctuating schedules and other things transpiring in his personal life.

The Listener told me that there were some pressing things in his life the he needed to work on and work out. He had to be healed and delivered in some areas of his life. He had to put things in proper perspective.

"God first, you second," he said. Of course, I did not like what I was hearing, I wanted what I wanted.

"Be patient, don't you want God's best?" he said, "God is working on me. God is working on you, and then when we come together, everything will be right. The way God intends it to be," he paused then continued, "let God work on me."

Inside I was frustrated. The very next day, I was at home taking a bath and I heard in my spirit, "selfish". I paused in thought. I heard, in my spirit," from the day I sent the Listener to you, he has been there for you and you can't do the same for him?" I immediately got out of the bathtub, I started to cry. I was convicted. I called the Listener and told him what happened. What God revealed to me in my spirit. I apologized to him for thinking only of myself. After I got off the phone, I prayed to God to remove the spirit of selfishness out of me. To help me not to be self-centered, thinking only of myself.

> *Prayer*
> *Father, you have made me aware of the selfish spirit that I was operating in. Father, I decree and declare that this selfish spirit has to go now, In the name of Jesus! Father, strengthen me. Less of me and more of you. I call forth the awareness and discernment, so that I am able to recognize, the when, what, and where that is happening around me. I do not want to think highly of myself. Father, keep me humble and meek, for I can do nothing without you, nor am I anything without you Lord. In Jesus Name Amen!!!*

My selfishness was actually tied to impatience. When we ask God to move in our lives, to have His way with us, we need to stay out of God's way. Let God be God. Stop putting God in a box, like a prize in the Cracker Jack box. When I used to eat Cracker Jacks, I would eat the popcorn until I reached the prize. Sometimes you waste the popcorn because you're anxious to get the prize and when the prize is not pleasing, you throw it all away.

Really, you were never interested in eating the popcorn, you were just interested in the prize. We put God in a box that we made too small for him. It has limits and we serve a limitless God. If God has made us a promise, He is a God that cannot and will not lie. He is called faithful, so He is faithful. Lord, help your people to be patient in the waiting process. Lord, you said to wait on you according to Psalms 27:14 (KJV), Wait on the Lord; be of good courage, and He shall strengthen thine heart; wait, I say, on the Lord.

We did not create God, God created us. He knows what we need, what needs to happen in our lives before we realize it. In the background was like He and I were in a long-distance relationship. The Listener was in the distant background. The Listener knew that my feelings were growing for him and so did I. Because this was something I was totally not use to, not being closer to someone I liked. I wanted to see him often, but God knew what was best for me and also, I needed to learn how to step out of the way, let go and let God, to see the prayers that I was praying to God manifest themselves in Gods timing and not mine. When I try to make things work, I fail at it, but I can do all things through Christ, who strengthens me. When God is in it, it works.

> *Wait and hope for and expect the Lord; be brave and of good courage and let your heart be stout and enduring. Yes, wait for and hope for and expect the Lord.*
> —Psalm 27:14 (AMP)

> *To everything there is a season, and a time for every matter or purpose under heaven*
> —Ecclesiastes 3:1 (AMP)

> *He has made everything beautiful in its time. He also has planted eternity in men's hearts and minds [a divinely implanted sense of a purpose working through ages which nothing under the sun but God alone can satisfy], yet so that men cannot find out what God has done from the beginning to the end.*
> —Ecclesiastes 3:11(AMP)

For every purpose and matter has its [right] time and judgment, although the misery and wickedness of man lies heavily upon him [who rebels against the king].
—Ecclesiastes 8:6 (AMP)

The Lord is good to those who wait hopefully and expectantly for Him, to those who seek Him [inquire of and for Him and require Him by right of necessity and on the authority of God's word]. It is good that one should hope in and wait quietly for the salvation (the safety and ease) of the Lord.
—Lamentations 3:25.26(AMP)

For the revelation awaits an appointed time; it speaks of the end and will not prove false. Though it lingers, wait for it; it will certainly come and will not delay.
—Habakkuk 2:3 (NIV)

Chapter 27

I Didn't Understand The Journey

When God made Eve as a helper, a suitable mate for Adam, she was equipped with everything that she needed to operate, function, and communicate with Adam. Adam and Eve were equally yoked. I needed to get myself together so that I could become the woman of God, who God intended me to be. To be equipped for modern day Adam that found me. People around me, friends or family, at times would ask me who I was seeing. Where was my man? Why is your man not around? Have I heard from the Listener? I was in constant communication with the Listener the way it should have been for me, so I could get my life on track. Thank God for delivering me from the opinions of others and that I keep unnecessary individuals out of my personal business. Everybody is not going to understand your journey. Everybody has a different path that they must take. I am not trying to walk anyone else's path. I only want to walk the path God has planned for me.

A spiritual journey is a phrase used by many different religions to mean the natural progression of a person as they grow in understanding of God, the world and himself. It is an intentional lifestyle of growing deeper in knowledge and wisdom. (Got questions.org)

The meaning of a journey is an act of travelling from one place to another. It also means; a long and often difficult process of personal change and development. I did not understand this journey I was on. James Allen wrote in his book *"As A Man Thinketh,"* and I will quote, *"As a man thinketh in his heart so is he," not only embraces the whole of a man's being, but is so comprehensive as to reach out to every condition and circumstance of his life.*

A man is literally what he thinks, his character being the complete sum of all thoughts. I had to learn to see myself the way God sees me. I was seeing the positive changes happening in my life and a lot of growth along the way. Nothing was laid out for me to know how life was going to go for me on this journey. It did not feel good all the time. It did not look or sound good at times. Even though the Listener knew my feelings were growing for him, he never gave me false hope and dreams. He did not play mind games. He respected all my decisions. He understood that I wanted to be in a relationship blessed by God. I was able to be transparent with the Listener. He made no definite promises and I am truly grateful for that.

We should never make promises that we cannot keep. I thank God now that the Listener was distant at times because it gave me time to reflect on conversations that we had about my children, raising my self-esteem, or having patience. We even had conversations on learning how to let go of things I did not have the ability to handle and give what I could not handle to God. I learned to trust God, learned how to build my confidence, learned how to trust my own decisions and much more. These things could not have been accomplished without God intervening.

The Listener was not in my face 24/7 because that was not what would have helped me. It would have been a distraction. All my focus would have been on the relationship, trying to please the Listener and sacrificing myself in the process. I did not know any other way to be. I would have not grown or healed, like I have in so many areas of my life. Isolation, in this case, helped me deal with self. It gave me solitude, where I could find out who I was. Learn to love myself, the beautiful creation that God had created, for the purpose to give Him glory, not man. How can I began to love anyone with the love I am supposed to love them with, if I do not know how to do just that? The Listener always pointed me in the direction of God. This was a good thing because God needed to be my focus.

Like I said earlier, I would try to give the Listener thanks. He would always say that it was not him, it's God. Thank God, not him. It has been four years of clean up for thirty-years plus of issues. I thought it was the devil in the way at times, or my flesh in the way. My life was out of order, but through the process of time, my prayers were being answered, just not in the way I would have thought they would have been answered. Lord, I see you now operating in my life. Lord, I see you. I see that you were trying to get my attention. You were trying to get me to look to you and not for my dad. Lord, you showed me that you are the answer to everything I have need of now and forever more. You may be reading this book and saying to yourself, you know God is all of these titles, but I had to learn of Him.

God is answered prayer in the form of:

> **Prosperity**
> **Protector**
> **Joy**
> **Time**
> **Patience**
> **Present Help**
> **Peace**
> **Friend of the friendless**
> **Strength**
> **Lamb of God**
> **Ruler Over All**
> **Faith**
> **Lord of Lords**
> **Elohim**
> **King of Kings**
> **Love**
> **Alpha and Omega**
> **My Healer**
> **My Covering**
> **My Judge**
> **My Father**
> **My Husband**
> **My Counselor**
> **My Teacher**

My Mother
My Comforter
My Deliverer
My Provider
My Friend
My Lawyer
My Creator
My Psychologist

I can go on and on, because now I understand that while I was looking for my dad, I should have been looking to the Father. All the answers, to every possible equation in life, all the answers were not out looking for my dad. My dad could not help himself, so how was He going to help me? I wish I knew then what I know now, that I should have been looking to the Father. God is creator of all and that makes Him all in all. The Lord will work things out in your life, if you allow him. You can never know Him if you do not try to develop a relationship with him. I say this because this was my journey to learn of the Father, have a relationship with the Father. This was a journey for me to see that while I was looking for my dad, I should have been looking to the Father. This has been a journey worth taking. Trust God on your journey.

Your life is a journey you must travel with a deep consciousness of God. It cost God plenty to get you out of that dead-end, empty-headed life you grew up in. He paid with Christ's sacred blood, you know. He died like an unblemished, sacrificial lamb, And this was no afterthought. Even though it has only lately-at the end of the ages- become public knowledge, God always knew he was going to do this for you. It is because of this sacrificed Messiah, whom God then raised from the dead and glorified, that you trust God, that you know you have a future in God.1Peter 1:18-21(MSG)

Our life is like a land journey; too even and easy and dull over long distances across the plains, too hard and painful up the steep grades; but on the summits of the mountain, you have a magnificent view—and feel

exalted—and your eyes are full of happy tears —you must continue your journey—you begin climbing down the other side, so busy with your footholds that your summit experience is forgotten.
   -Lloyd Douglas

The journey between what you once were and who you are now becoming is where the dance of life really takes place. -Barbara DeAngelis

Chapter 28
Explaining The Baggage

Do you remember when I was explaining about the baggage I was carrying around with me? Well, allow me to explain how I actually unpacked each baggage. In the process of the Listener keeping his distance, I began by praying to God to show me myself. I wanted to know the bad and the ugly parts of me. When you pray a prayer like that, you need to be ready to accept what God is going to reveal to you about yourself. It was the cold hard truth, which I could not deny. Once I digested the truth about myself, I began to ask God to forgive me. I asked the Lord to help me fix these issues. I asked God to create in me a clean heart and to renew a right spirit in me that was in right standing with God. I asked God to remove everything that is hindering me from serving him in truth and everything that is not like Him. I would say constantly; "LESS OF ME, LORD! AND MORE OF YOU, LORD! This was a process and this process was going to take TIME.

During the time, I had prayer from those who were close to me and wanted to see me healed, and set free. My mother was praying for me, the Listener, my sisters, and friends that were prayer warriors, were praying for me. I needed people, who would take out the time to pray for me. They were always saying encouraging words, not words to tear me down and discourage me. The positive feedback was great, especially when I was saying things that were contrary to what the Word of God said. I loved it, because it kept me on my toes.

The first major baggage that I had to get through was being an enabler. I believe that all enablers can learn from the story of the prodigal son. When the father gave his son his inheritance and let him go on his merry way, he did not run after him from what is said in the Bible.

He did not beg and plead for him to stop what he was about to do. This also shows me that it does not matter your station in life, rich or poor, the prodigal son comes from all walks of life. The prodigal son's drive to fulfill a desire to run with the wrong crowd, use drugs, steal, be dependent on others to do for them and more, hold a lot of consequences. The Father did not blame himself for the prodigal son's behavior; he just allowed life to take its course. When we interfere in what God is doing in others lives, whether we view it as bad or just a struggle, I believe we hinder the inevitable. We prolong their situation because we try to fix things.

In the Bible, we could assume that the father truly loved the prodigal son and prayed for his son to come back home and get his life back on track. Maybe, the father had faith in God that God was going to heal his son's mind and deliver him. Maybe God had answered the father's prayers, and the father was so excited that his prayers were answered, that he had decided upon the celebration of his son's return. I know this event increased that father's faith in God. Could it be that this miracle was for the people to see so that they would believe in God?

The results of the father not being an enabler allowed his son to hit rock bottom. The son figured things out, apologized, and asked for forgiveness. The prodigal son came back humble and was willing to work for his father even though his father had the means to provide for him. Now enablers are not exclusive to being an enabler to family members only. Some enablers are enablers to friends, their children, boyfriends, girlfriends, even spouses in my opinion. Some people in my opinion have a tendency to play the victim, which I will refer to them as the needy. The statements they make start with, "<u>I can't</u>," "<u>I don't have</u>," "<u>What had happened was</u>," "<u>Somebody took</u>," "<u>Can you help me out?</u>" "<u>Do you have</u>?" "<u>I am having a hard time</u>," "I think you understand what I am trying to say."

It is a very negative disposition. You begin to live their lives. You are not living the life you want to live, or doing the things you want to do because every time you turn around, you are helping the needy. You start putting yourself to the side, your dreams to the side, even your desires to the side. You begin making excuses, saying that the needy really need this more than I do. I can wait because they need me. But while you are consumed with them, time begins to stand still for you because you have convinced yourself that what you want is not that important. The needy, has now become your stumbling block, the mountains, the stones blocking your destiny. You are not moving forward.

Again, I was an enabler to certain family members. This was your family, Kim? Yes, this was my family. Blood is thicker than water, Kim. Yes, blood is thicker than water, but all blood types are not the same, even though we are family.

How did you accomplish this seemingly difficult task? I am glad you asked that question. There comes a time when you have to shake the dust from your feet. You shake the dust because you cannot make people do the right thing, or do what is best for them. The needy is always looking for a handout, or always looking for someone to rescue them from their problems they put themselves in, just playing the victim role. They are a victim because they choose to be a victim. I will say this again; Life Is about Choices! We have to choose even if we are a victim of circumstances; we have to choose and refuse to not be a victim anymore. I had a hard time with this baggage.

Kim, how did you stop being the enabler? I accomplished this by determining in my mind, if the issue that was being brought before me, answered these questions. Was it my business? Was it my doing that put them in this situation? Could I fix the issue? Do I want to fix this issue? Or, I would ask God if I needed to respond to the issues the needy were having? In not being so quick to respond, I was able to realize that if I keep coming to the rescue of everyone else, it was going to slowly take the life out of me. The well that was full was going to eventually run dry.

All you are doing for the person that you are an enabler to is crippling them. Why was I coming to the rescue of people who were capable of making decisions and fending for themselves? If I was to go home and be with the Father in Glory, guess what? They would have to figure things out, or ask someone else. Certain family members came to me out of habit. I opened this door and they had figured me out. They knew if they pulled at my heartstrings, then I would say, "Yes." I carried my heart around on my sleeves, open and exposed. I had to learn how to say "NO!" I would get in the mirror and practice the word no in different voices, which I owe a special thanks to God for putting that on my pastor's heart to say in a sermon he was preaching one Sunday morning.

No, I am not coo coo for Coco Puffs. I know it sounds crazy, but it is so true. Kim, you said this was a habit, so this had to be real tough for you? Yes, it was tough, I would cry or feel bad sometimes, and they would not know it, but I had to help myself. You cannot be afraid to say, "No," or worry about how the other person is going to feel. That is selfish for the needy to assume that you are going to do something for them, and they are not concerned about how it is going to affect you.

The fact that I was an enabler was killing me. Guess what? They did not, get mad all the time, or hate me, for telling them no. It is not what you say, but how you say it. Let me even go a step further. If they were to get mad, so what? You are entitled to say, "No." The first word we learn besides Momma and Daddy is no. We learn no before yes and for the life of me, I do not understand how we got to the point in life that we fear to say no.

The needy had figured things out on their own, and I was no longer weighted down with their problems. People do not like to hear the word, "No," but it is a part of life. I remember one day I was home and got two phone calls, back-to-back, from two male associate friends. I knew they liked me, but I had made it clear friendship was as far as we could go. The first guy I will refer to as "Only Hears Himself," and the other I spoke to you about earlier in the book, who I refer to as "Never Moves Forward." The conversation went like this:

"Hey. sis," Only Hears Himself said.

"Hey," I said, greeting him.

"So what's been going on?" he said curiously.

"Just trying to stay focused." I was wondering where this conversation was going.

"Same here. So, what have you been up to?" he said enthusiastically.

"Have you been going out? Getting out of the house?" He was being nosey.

"Yes, I get out," I responded in an agitated tone.

"Where have you been going?"?,

"Why all the questions?" I was ready to shut him down.

"I just was trying to see what you have been up to. Has your man been taking you out?" He was trying to figure out if I am involved with someone.

"That is none of your business," I said sarcastically with an attitude.

He said, "I am sorry. I didn't mean any harm. I just was concerned. You know you are like a sister to me." I know he did not mean any harm. He was just trying to get information.

The conversation was not going anywhere. Then he proceeded to ask me if I could go anywhere with my significant other for three days, where would I go? I told him on a cruise. He asked me if I had ever been on a cruise before, and my response was no. Then he says "Well, in August, my family is taking a cruise. Would you like to go?"

"No," I said quickly because that was not going to happen.

"No!" he repeated in shock.

"Yes. No!" I said firmly.

"Are you serious?" He was shocked at my response.

"Most definitely." I knew he wanted to be in an intimate setting with me and that was out of the question.

He says, "Why not?"

"You are not my significant other. I am your sister, remember?" I basically gave him back his own words.

"That sure is cold," he remarked, upset by my response.

"Well, let me ask you this?" he said because he only hears himself.

"How about I come and take you out to dinner—just the two of us?"

"No," I said. (He does not get it.)

"No!"! he said as if he is still shocked.

"Yes, no," I said firmly.

He said, "What is wrong with dinner?"

"You are more than welcome to invite me to breakfast or maybe a lunch, but dinner is reserved for a man that is interested in me and I in him, or a special man in my life, Now if it is going to be a group of mutual friends and family. then cool".

"Man!" He sounded frustrated.

It had not been an hour that I had been off the phone and the phone rang again. This was "Never Moves Forward" calling me now.

"Hello," I said.

"Hi, Kim. How are you?" Never Moves Forward said.

"I am fine and yourself," I answered pleasantly.

"I am good," he said with assurance.

"I wanted to know if we could go out to dinner and spend some time together."

I immediately said, "No."

, "No! Why not?" He spoke with sudden anger.

"I do not want you to get the wrong impression, we can go to breakfast or lunch, but not dinner, that is reserved for my significant other."

"That's messed up!"He was annoyed.

"Well, that is the way I see it," I said firmly.

Never Moves Forward was very upset from the response he received from me, but he still communicates with me. My point is learning to say no is very liberating. Walk to the beat of your own drum. Don't allow someone to make you feel guilty for saying no, if you really do not want to do something. Please do not be the doormat that people are constantly walking over, or a wasteland where everyone comes and dumps their garbage. The smell of garbage is disturbing, and I am sure if you stay in the wasteland, you will eventually smell too. Why? Because you will be carrying around all their garbage and your own garbage with you. I was there, and thank God I have grown out of it.

The next form of baggage I had to overcome was low self-esteem. The low self-esteem was a lot of work. I did not love myself. The love that friends and family had for me was not going to help my low self-esteem.

When you do not love yourself, you will believe all the negative things other people say, along with the negative things you believe about yourself. When you do not love yourself, your conversation is very negative, and you inherit a complaining spirit. Nothing is good enough or right.

I was overweight. I was home from a work injury, and I had limited abilities that kept me in sort of an isolated situation. When you are unable to participate in leisure activities, it seems like every type of event is happening around you. It is like when you decide to go on a diet, everyone wants ice cream. They want to bake or buy pastries. Everything you are not suppose to have is at your fingertips. It seemed like everybody was taking amazing trips, everybody was having parties, and everybody was going to amusement parks, while I was at home, unable to partake. My self-esteem was already bad after my marriage. After dealing with the Forgery, it was worse. To top it off, when the Listener told me to air out, I was practically a basket case with low self-esteem.

Did the Forgery cause your low self-esteem? No, the Forgery was not the cause of my low self-esteem. He never complained about how I looked. I felt that, because things did not work out for us, it was because I was fat, or not pretty enough.

You know you can be your worst enemy and you are definitely your own worst critic. That was the furthest thing from the truth. When the Listener came along and said to air out, I figured, Oh, Boy! (sadly) *This is his way out. He does not want to be bothered with me now that I am injured. Besides, I am too young and too fat for him. He is just trying to be nice.* That was not true. The problem was in my head.

I remember one day being out with the Listener, and he had his camera. He wanted to take some pictures of me, but I refused. He asked me why? I began to tell him that I did not like the way I looked in pictures. He tried to encourage me, but I had the problem. I said, " I do not like taking pictures."

He said, "But you are beautiful."

I said, "Well, I do not like the way I look in pictures."

After that day, I thought about that conversation often. I found this scripture in the Bible and began to quote it.

Who satisfies your youth [your necessity and desire at your personal age and situation] with good so that your youth, renewed, is like the eagle's [strong, overcoming, soaring]
Psalm 103:5 (AMP)

I usually just say, "Thank you, Lord, that you renew my youth like the eagles." I still say it to this day.

One of my daughters came to me and said, "Mom, why don't you take pictures? We need to take some pictures together."

I told her I did not like the way I looked on pictures. It would stay on my mind what my daughter and the Listener said, so one day while I was in my room, I looked in the mirror and I did not like what I saw. I said, "Lord, help me to get this weight off me. Direct me as to what to do." I started to say, "Lord, I thank you that I am a healthy one hundred and thirty pounds and in great health."

This was my faith confession. I would say this over again and I still say it over and over because I still believe that I will reach my goal. I lost 56 pounds in a year and to God be the Glory! Then I decided to do my hair, makeup, and pretend I was at a photo shoot here at the house with my smart phone. I took so many pictures with my phone. All the photos I took I decided to send to the Listener. He always said positive comments that made me feel good. He was the only one I was sending the pictures to for a while. Don't ask me why because I cannot tell you. I then posted the pictures he liked on social media.

I received a lot of positive feedback. This continued until one day I was tired of taking pictures. I did not feel a need to take another picture, and anytime family and friends were taking pictures, I no longer said no. The low self-esteem was over. I asked God to help me, show me how to love myself. How can we say we love others, if we do not love ourselves? I had to come to realize that I mattered. I am important. I am not concerned whether I am important to anyone else. The only thing that is important is that God loves me and I love me. Knowing what God says about me and how he sees me is what truly matters. Knowing this determines the direction my life will take. Low self-esteem is no longer a part of me.

Okay, we talked about the baggage of an enabler, and low self-esteem. The baggage of passiveness was work because I did not realize I was allowing things to slide that I should have addressed. I especially should have addressed with my kids. I think because I did not want to argue or get upset about little trivial things. I would rather be silent than to respond, maybe the situation would go away. What came to mind is that I am a letter being read by all. What I mean, is that I am being watched and I truly did not want my kids to become what I was, or losing respect for me because of being passive about things. Through the eyes of my children, they needed to see me as strong. They needed to know by my actions that you do not run from problems or certain situations.

How could my children know how to stand, when I was not standing? I was running. I now address things that are a concern for me. I stand up for what is right, even if I choose not to deal with it. I was being perceived as weak, and one of my daughters lost respect for me, watching me to allow people to run all over me. Thank God that my daughter opened up to me to tell me how she felt so we could both heal. We have a better relationship now.

How did I overcome the baggage of dishonesty, along with distrust, when I was thinking all men were the same? I felt that men said one thing, but always meant something else. It seemed like every man that I was running into was shallow.

Unfortunately, the men that I was running into would get what they wanted and move on. I guess you can say I was being judgmental. The problem was not them; it was me. In order to stop the cycle, I had to change me. In the beginning, I had a smart tongue. I was sarcastic, and I was mean. I was taking things out on the Listener for what other men had done to me. The Listener actually had had his full one day and told me he did not have to take the treatment I was dishing out to him. He told me that he did not hurt me, mistreat me, and so do not take out on him what other men had done to me. Man! The way he said it, made me get some get-right in less than sixty seconds. I cleaned up my act really quick and apologized. He was right. I put myself in his shoes and realized that I would not have wanted someone to do me that way. No time to be reaping bad seeds. Misery may love company, but I am not trying to meet misery, much less get to know misery. I am learning to trust my instincts, be honest to myself and others. I learned to not judge people, especially prematurely.

Let's talk about the baggage of promiscuity. The result of my promiscuity stemmed from fear. The fear I had was a result of the rape. I was having sex out of fear, not for an enjoyment.

> *What I feared has come upon me; what I dreaded has happened to me. I have no peace, no quietness; I have no rest, but only turmoil.*
>
> —Job 3:25,26 (NIV)

Dr. Phil's advice under life strategies on his web page said, "Your past easily becomes your future because what you fear, you create. If you feel deprived of some experience, or emotion from someone else, give yourself emotional closure. Give yourself what you didn't get from someone else now. Create what you want out of life. If you want to be loved, be loveable. If you want to get your family interested in your life, get interested in their lives."

Oswald Chambers said, "The remarkable thing about God is that when you fear God, you fear nothing else, whereas if you do not fear God, you fear everything else."

In retrospect, I was young, fearful, having sex and did not have a clue as to what I was doing. Things just were going downhill fast. I got pregnant and did not know. By the time I found out, I was about sixteen to eighteen weeks. I know you are wondering how could I not know? I was flat as a pancake in my stomach, I had a six pack. I was running track, and I trusted that the individual I had had sex with pulled out in time. He told me that is what he did. I had an abortion that almost cost me my life, but thank God, I am still here. At age eighteen, I got pregnant again. I wanted to keep the baby. The guy that was the father told me I was not going to keep it. He was going to pay for the abortion. He told me if I tried to have the baby, he would hate me, and I was too afraid of what that hate was going to entail.

I got the abortion. Like he said, he paid for it. However, after I got the abortion, he broke up with me. I found out later that he had another girl pregnant at the same time.

Next, I started dating this thirty-five-year-old man, and I had no problem with it because I felt that at his age he should have been ready to settle down. I thought that he was mature because he was older. Wrong! Surely, this was going to be it. I was going to be in secure hands. I got pregnant by him. I did not even know I was pregnant. I had not gained any weight; I did not have a rock-hard stomach; it was just soft. He had a sixteen-year-old daughter. He was not married and I thought things were well between the two of us. I remember calling him, excited to tell him the news. I had made up in my mind that I was going to go through with this pregnancy, no more abortions, and if he did not want to take care of this responsibility with me, then I would do it by myself.

When I told him, he was in shock. He was telling me that I was not ready to have any kids. He told me how he was struggling to take care of his sixteen-year-old daughter. I told him that I understood, and that it would be no problem. I would work hard to take care of the baby, I will get a place of my own, but I wanted my baby. The next day he called me and told me that I need to make an appointment to get an abortion, I was not having this baby and before I get to far long, he was taking me to get rid of the baby. I could not get in a word at all. He would not listen to me. I got the silent treatment. I wanted him to know how far along I was, but he did not want to hear anything. I had the abortion, and he dumped me. I did not want to speak to him again. I was almost seventeen weeks when I had that abortion.

Three years later he ran into my little brother, wanting to know how I was doing. When my brother came to tell me, he gave him my phone number, I was so upset, but the number had already been given out. When he called me, he wanted to come see me. I let him. We got into this heated conversation, because he wanted to start seeing me again. I told him that I cannot because of what he did to me. I told him that our baby would have been three years old. He told me to stop tripping. I was only a couple of weeks pregnant. I went off. I told him for his information, had he listened to me, he would have known I was over sixteen weeks pregnant. He told me I was not. I asked him did he want to see the proof. He said that if he had known that I was that far gone, he would have not had me get an abortion. He said besides, you were not big, you did not look like you were that far gone. I said I was and you made me get rid of my baby. I told him that every time I see him I remember what he did to me and I can't seem to get pass that. He said he was sorry, but the damage was already done.

The listener helped me with this baggage when he told me to air out. The Listener said that I did not need to be intimate with any man. I have to be honest now, I did not like that, nor was I accustomed to it at all. I desired to be with the Listener and yet the doors were closed. Were the doors opened in the beginning with the Listener Kim? Yes, they were opened.

I asked the Listener one day if he would show me what my first time was supposed to be like. I remember the silence on the phone. You could have cut the silence with a knife. I was asking something big. He said, yes he would. That experience erased the rape completely in my mind.

I understood at that moment that all men are not the same. I am not condoning sex before marriage. I am not saying what we did was the right thing to do. I know some people feel like they need to test the waters before hand, but if you test the waters be prepared for whatever the consequences are. I believe that we serve a God that is bigger than what we can ever imagine and we can ask him for what we want and he will do better than that. I just know that my past has been erased and after that event between the Listener and I, the doors were closed. I made it through three months of celibacy. The three months turned into eight months and I have been blessed to have made it to a little more than three years' abstinence. With the Listener respecting me, I began to respect myself. The more I focused on God the more I desired to be obedient to God's Word. I remember when I had called the Listener to talk to him.

I told him that I do not want to sleep around until I am married to the man of God that God the Father has for me. I want my relationship blessed. I want God's best. I like not following my flesh, giving in to my flesh. I believe God knows me well enough to supply all my needs. It is a time and a place for everything and I like living in the blessed and preserved section.

When my husband finds me, he will find a good and preserved thing. I did not really think this was possible. I feel like I have been given an amazing opportunity to start my life all over again. A relationship built on sex or looks is no relationship at all to me. What happens when the youthful beauty has gone? Will you still love me? If for some reason you or I are not able to have sex as often as we use to or at all, Will you still love me? The covenant that we are bound to, will we still honor it and give each other our best? Will you still love me like Christ loves the church? God first me second, for better or worse, will we pray our way through the good and bad times? Will you and I pray for each other even when we can't pray for ourselves? Do you understand that Satan believes in destroying family and he wants us to get caught up in the world and self to break the covenant we made?

Do you understand Prayer is essential for the survival of marriage? I understand this, that's why I rather wait on the Lord to send me my mate. I know a lady who was a virgin for over 30 years before she got married to a man of God that loved her and she loved him. They had their honeymoon, consummated the marriage. Shortly after the marriage her husband got into an accident. The injuries went from bad to worse. They had not been married long, I believe it was only two years and he died. The sex life was over I believe two months after the marriage. She did not run away. She did not go find someone else to sleep with because her husband could not be sexually active with her. She honored the covenant that she and her husband made, which is death do us part. I no longer carry the baggage of Promiscuity, by the grace of God. I am an over comer, by the blood of the lamb. I am grateful for God's healing power that has set me free. Who the Son sets free, is truly free in deed.

The baggage of failure was eliminated through prayer, a lot of positive reinforcement through my mother, sisters, prayer warriors, and God almighty leading me and directing what to say and do. I had to tell myself that I was not a failure, this tied in with me not knowing my self-worth. God did not make failures he made masterpieces. God is a master artist. He made all of us uniquely different. To the natural eye we may think we see flaws. But the flaws that the natural eyes see are not flaws. They are a mark of the true craftsmanship of God. The Bible says;

> *But you are a chosen people, a royal priesthood, a holy nation, God's special possession, that you may declare the praises of him who called you out of the darkness into his wonderful light. Once you were not a people of God, once you had not received mercy, but now you have received mercy.*
>
> —1Peter 2:9,10(NIV)

I can say now that I am not a failure, I am blessed by God. I am his treasure.

> *For you are a people holy to the Lord your God. The Lord your God has chosen you out of all the peoples on the face of the earth to be his treasured possession.*
>
> —Deuteronomy 7:6(NIV)

In the baggage of disappointment, I would always get disappointed every time things did not turn out the way I had expected them to. When someone said they were going to do something for me, take me somewhere, or were late, I would get so disappointed; I allowed it to ruin my day. When the relationships failed, I was disappointed. People could apologize, but I would not let it go. I found out that people make mistakes; things happen that are out of our control. When things did not turn out the way I expected, I need to let it go. Everything happens for a reason. I really realized that I had a problem when I went to my acupuncture appointment. I had been injured and was off from work for three years. I had gone to physical therapy, shockwave therapy, aqua therapy, all kinds of therapy. I was scheduled for so many visits and then it would be discontinued.

It seemed as though right when I was starting to get better the therapy was shut off, no more. This was frustrating for me because I wanted to get better. When I would go to the acupuncturist, I was feeling better after every session. I was finally sleeping through the night. The acupuncturist had prescribed some herbs to help me. Everything was great.

The nurse told me that I only had three visits left. When the acupuncturist came in to treat me, I told him what she said. He said, "Okay." I began to complain about the insurance company discontinuing the acupuncture services that were going so well for me. I talked about all the therapies I had had before this service, and how it seemed as though the service was interrupted as soon as I began to get better or get relief from the pain that I was suffering from. I had tears coming down my face.

He looked at me. "That is more than enough treatments you have had. If you were coming to me at my office, you would only be coming once or twice a month and yet you have had eighteen visits. You have had more than enough treatments.

You are healed. You have to stop what you are doing. You are releasing negative energy every time you finish therapy and those signals defeat the purpose for the therapy. It short stops your recovery, and it makes you sick."

This made sense because an acupuncturist focuses on energy and maintaining wellness in their patients." You have to think more positively, release everything to God, tell God that you release everything to him, and I will be praying for you". I love him for that. Thank you Lord for blessing me with an acupuncturist that believed in God and you sent me to him so that he could help me. I had to learn to look at the positive in every situation. I realized that I was not happy internally and that was the problem.

I was looking for happiness in others. I did not know how to make myself happy. I was looking for others to make me happy. I had to turn things around fast. I began trying to find things that made me happy. I had to find things I liked to do. I learned how not to be dependent on others and to depend on myself.

I now look for the positive in every negative situation. All relationships are going to end, either by death or separation. I learned that some relationships are seasonal and some relationships are covenant. When you understand this about relationships, you know where to place people in your life.

I pray that I have shed enough light on how I overcame my baggage. I am thankful for God's grace and mercy. God knew what and who I needed to get me through these stages of my life. To God be the glory!

Chapter 29

God Said, "Focus On Me, And I will Take Care Of Everything Else!"

In 2014, I was at home by myself. I was walking to the kitchen and the Spirit of God spoke in my spirit. He asked, "Do you remember the story of Peter?"

"Yes, Lord," I replied.

He continued, "When I was walking on the water and Peter was in the boat?

"Yes, Lord," I said again, recalling the story.

"When I told Peter to come to me and he started walking on the water to me, what happened?" He asked.

"Yes, Lord. He took his eyes off of you and began to sink."

God said, "Right, I need you to focus on me and I will take care of everything else around you."

"Okay, Lord,"

> *"If your first concern is to look after yourself, you'll never find yourself. But if you forget about yourself and look to me, you'll find both yourself and me."*
> —Matthew 10:39 9(MSG)

> *Only people who don't know God are always worrying about such things. Your Father knows what you need. But put God's work first, and these things will be yours as well.*
> —Luke 12:30,31(CEV)

Looking away [from all that will distract] to Jesus, Who is the Leader and Source of our faith [giving the first incentive for our belief] and is also its Finisher [bringing it to maturity and perfection]. He, for the joy [of obtaining the prize] that was set before Him, endured the cross, despising and ignoring the shame, and is now seated at the right hand of the throne of God.
—Hebrews 12:2 (AMP)

I thought I was doing just that. I thought I was focusing on God. I was reading the Word of God, praying, and going to church. God was leading me to read certain books that were helpful in my healing process. The messages that had been preached by my pastor at church, or the messages that were preached by guest pastors that my pastor invited to preach in his pulpit were always answers to my prayers, confirmations of something God was showing me in His Word, or telling me in my spirit. In order to receive, you have to have a receptive spirit, to be able to listen to what God is telling you do. The definition of a Listener is someone who pays attention, heeds; obeys. I needed to do all of this.

<u>It's A Good Thing to Hope for Help from God</u>

I'll never forget the trouble, the utter lostness, the taste of ashes, the poison I've swallowed. I remember it all--oh, well, I remember--the feeling of hitting the bottom. But there's one other thing I remember. I keep a grip on hope: God's loyal love couldn't have run out, His merciful love couldn't have dried up. They're created new every morning. How great your faithfulness! I'm sticking with God (I say it over and over). He's all I've got left.

God proves to be good to the man who passionately waits, to the woman who diligently seeks. It's a good thing to quietly hope, quietly hope for help from God. It's a good thing when you're young to stick it out through the

> hard times. When life is heavy and hard to take, go off by yourself. Enter the silence. Bow in prayer. Don't ask questions: Wait for hope to appear. Don't run from trouble. Take it full face. The worst is never the worst. Why? Because the Master won't ever walk out and fail to return. If he works severely, he works tenderly. His stockpiles of loyal love are immense. He takes no pleasure in making life hard, in throwing roadblocks in the way: Stomping down hard on luckless prisoners, Refusing justice to victims in the court of High God, Tampering with evidence- the Master does not approve of such things.
>
> —Lamentations 3:19-36 (MSG

It has taken a lot of years for me to get to this point. The Listener was brought into my life after all these years, to help me heal from my past wounds, to grow, and to start a new life. Although God placed the Listener in my life, I unintentionally was starting to put too much of my focus on the Listener and my trust was in him. My focus should have been on God and most certainly all my trust should have been in the Lord. The Listener was a man. Our trust is not to be placed in man. Trusting in man can not heal me, save me, nor deliver me; only God can heal, save, and deliver. Man makes mistakes and will disappoint you at times, and this is not always intentional, but God will never disappoint you or make a mistake about you.

> Thus says the Lord, "Cursed is the man who trusts in mankind and makes flesh his strength, And whose heart turns away from the Lord. For he will be like a bush in the desert and will not see when prosperity comes, But he will live in stony wastes in the wilderness, A land of salt without inhabitant.
>
> —Jeremiah 17:5,6 (NAS)

*Stop trusting in mere humans, who have but a breath in their nostrils. Why hold them in esteem?*Isaiah 2:22 (NIV)
—Psalm 146:3 (NIV)

To me, the Listener had become, and was, a wonderful person that I was trying to attach myself to. In my mind, he was the good that was substituting all the bad in my life from my past. Who could blame me? The problem was, how was I to know if I was making a decision based on solely emotions, and not with a clear and healed mind? The distance helped because it was more important to get to know who I was as a person, love God first and learn to love myself, which would help determine if my interest in him was true or not.

Chapter 30

He Sent An Earthquake To Get My Attention

God is a jealous God. He expects exclusive devotion to Him. God never left me in the dark. He never leaves his children in the dark. He will shine the light. He sends the warning signs. There are consequences for not listening. I did not take heed to the warning signs and God shook things up in my life.

Looking back over the years, there were times when God was trying to get my attention, trying to get me to focus on Him. He was trying to get me to understand that He wanted and needed to be the head of my life, the center of my heart and my focus point. In November 20, 2005, I was diagnosed with walking pneumonia. I was out of commission for about 3 to 6 weeks. I started reading the word of God and praying, until I went back to work. July 25, 2009, I was having problems with outlet dysfunction.

I started back reading my Bible and praying and when I went back to work I had excuses why I could not read my Bible or pray as much anymore. May 10, 2010, I was off of work for foot surgery. I still was not cooperative. These were earthquakes, not major earthquakes, but they shook enough to get my attention temporarily. I would have considered them major earthquakes because of how they affected me at that particular time when it occurred. In fact, I do not know anyone that has experienced a real earthquake and it does not get their attention.

An earthquake is defined as a sudden and violent shaking of the ground, sometimes causing great destruction, as a result of movements within the earth's crust or volcanic action. Let me explain what was taking place around this time before the actual earthquake.

My foundation was not fully built on the rock. My foundation was some rock and some sand. If my life, which is my foundation is not built on solid ground, which is Christ, then I have a foundation that is sure to fail. The Bible tells us that all other ground is sinking sand. The earthquakes that were causing movement in my foundation, were not real big, but it was supposed to get my attention. What was suppose to direct me back to Christ, was not doing it for me completely. I had to have wake-up calls, I was alerted, but for some reason, I would go back to some of the old ways. Please do not get me wrong, I was not getting weaker, I was getting stronger, I was eliminating things as the earthquakes happened, but it was time for an all or nothing revelation. I could not serve God and self. God was not going to play half a part in my life. I wanted my prayers answered, right? In order for this to happen a major shifting in my foundation needed to happen. This earthquake was the big one. The one that was going to destroy strongholds, generational curses, this earthquake was going to break up all the fallow ground, which it did.

The Listener's mother had been suffering from an illness that made him and his siblings come to a decision to place her in a facility that she could be taken care of properly, while being treated for her illnesses at the same time. One day the Lord came and had taken the Listener's mom home to glory. The night before the Listener's mom passed away, I had trouble sleeping. I could not understand why, so I began to pray until I could go to sleep. The next morning, I had awakened about ten in the morning. I laid in the bed. I said, "Thank you Lord, for waking me up today." I was quiet and I looked over to the right side of me and my phone was on my bed. I decided to go on my social media page to see what was going on. Social media is like the news. Whether you want to know something or not it will be reported or shown.

It is really worse than the news at times because some of the local broadcasters had no filter. Local broadcasters? Yes, every individual that has a social media page are what I call the local broadcasters. Some of the local broadcasters, broadcast their lives, their personal business, their activities, their gossip, you name it, it is on social media, one of the new forms of communication. You could even call it a tracker, away to find out where people are located. This can be said to be another form of a lojack device. Once I got on the social media, I noticed that the Listener had posted on his page a request for prayer because he had just received the devastating news that his mother had passed away. I was in such a shock.

I started crying, saying, "Oh Lord, what should I say or do?" I left a comment on his page. What came to me to say on his page at that time was something like; "God sent an angel to the earth to take care of you and your siblings. God equipped this angel with everything she needed to take care of you and your siblings.

Then the angel got sick and God needed someone to take care of his angel, so He asked you and your siblings to take care of His angel until he called her back home to be with Him."

It was something like that. Moving forward, I felt so helpless.

I called my family that knew of the Listener and told them what happened. Crying, I called one of my relatives. I told my relative what happened on the phone and what I did.

"No, Kim," my relative said, "not on social media. You call him and talk to him. That social media is so impersonal."

I was so out of it. I felt as though I was in sort of a freeze mode. I clarified to my relative that I was not trying to do that; that was not my intentions. I did not want to be impersonal. I honestly, just did not know what to say.

My relative got off the phone with me and before she hung up the phone she said to call the Listener. I did just that reluctantly. The phone ranged and he picked up the phone. It was silent. I knew he was on the phone. I asked the Listener was he okay. I apologized for his loss of his mother. I explained to the Listener that I had gone on social media that morning. My mind was scattering around, trying to say the right words to him. I knew this was a delicate situation and surely I did not want to offend him, or seem callus. I explained that after I had seen his post, I had to call. I asked him, was there anything that I could do for him.

In a very quiet, shocked and hurtful voice, he said, "No, I am okay."

To me, no, no, no, he was not okay and was not going to be okay for a while. I am not saying that he would have not been productive, or unable to take care of his responsibilities, that is not what I was saying. He is not a man that is going to just sit around. For the Listener, I knew that he would immediately go back to work and try to keep himself busy, which he was trying to do, but that does not take the hurt away, the emptiness away, the loneliness away that he was going to go through. I offered to go over and be there for him, to sit with him, to be quiet, and listen if he wanted to talk: to just be there. The Listener said, "No, I will be okay." I reiterated, that I did not mind, I was home with an injury. I had been home since 2012 from a work-related injury.

I had partially torn my meniscus and I was on crutches. I was on crutches for two years and seven months and a year and three months on a cane. Everything that could possibly hurt, hurt. I had been going through a snake and crocodile swamp, waiting for my job's insurance to help me. I was denied an appointment to see a surgeon, then denied surgery once I finally saw the surgeon, I was continuously denied medication to help me with pain. The Listener was their helping me along with my dad, my dad's wife, and my cousin, by giving me pain medications to get me through the day and nights. They were all trying to help me. It was an experience that I would not wish on my worst enemy. The Listener was concerned about me getting rest because I would be up for two to three days suffering. He even went so far as to take the time to wash my clothes, to make sure I had clean clothes. I told the Listener that even though I was injured, I still could be there for him. I could be there in whatever capacity he needed. To be honest, it really was not much that I could physically do, my heart and mind was in the right place, but my body was not. I was making a decision based on emotions, not thought out, nor a sound decision.

Did you ever get the surgery, Kim? Yes, praise God, I finally got the surgery. My knee is doing wonderful. The surgery was an hour. An hour long procedure, can you believe that? I was waiting three years to get a surgery that only took an hour to do. You want to know the crazy part? The insurance company still denied me medication to take after the surgery. I never knew so much cruelty existed. This has been a horrific experience as far as my knee goes, but it has been a liberating experience for me as far as my healing goes. I was sat down to get cleaned up, washed up, to be made whole by the Father. It would have been more challenging if I was working still, but I had to be sat down to learn how to listen to God, know His voice, and walk in His grace and mercy.

Back to the story; after I told him that I could be there for him, in whatever capacity he needed,I reassured him, "I love you, Listener."

"I know you love me, but it is okay," he said.

Before, I finish this part of the story; I need you to understand some things.

Chapter 31

There Are Two Sides In A Battle

Two sides were in battle. One side of the battle was my flesh and the other side of the battle was my spirit man. I say this because I want you to see both sides at work, but God will ultimately get the glory. This is what I guess would be called, setting up the stage. Earlier in the book, I told you that the Listener was a God sent. He was sent to help me unpack my baggage. Remember, I mentioned that after the Listener and I had been communicating for awhile, he realized that I was broken and needed to air out? And also, that I did not need to be in an intimate relationship, really not any relationship because I had a lot of healing that needed to take place and he was going to stay in the background? He never promised me anything.

It was not ever established that we were an exclusive couple, much less a couple at all. In my mind, I had a totally different story. He was such a breath of fresh air with so many wonderful qualities, and he had a beautiful relationship with the Lord, that I could not help but fall for him. He felt that I needed to get myself together because I was a shipwreck on a distant island [A figure of speech]. I was not used to being single, set apart.

God had come to the rescue me. This was not going to be an overnight success. This was going to take some work. Allow me to give you an example of what was going on in the back ground with me. It is like an ice sculpturing contest. One of the contestants has a block of ice to sculpt out—as a lion sculpture—as his design of choice.

In the process, something goes wrong. Part of the ice breaks off, seemingly to ruin the design. The contestant has to reconfigure how to still create the design, in spite of the broken part. He has to go about it a different way than was expected, but in the end the design was created. Not only was the lion created, but it was better than the original lion sculpture design of choice. God is the sculpture in this analogy and I am the block of ice.

Remember, I told you I use to go from one relationship to the next. Okay, let's get back to the story. He told me that he knew I loved him, but he was okay. I got off the phone with him. Three days later, I was concerned.

I was trying to communicate; I was trying to find out where to send cards and flowers to show respect and love. I was feeling helpless and left out of the loop here. Here is a man that I have grown to love and I want to be there for him and I am feeling as though I have been pushed completely out of the picture. My flesh is rising now. I am not praying about it, I am not asking God about it. I decided to call up a relative of mine, which I will refer to as One-View. I talked to One-View about the situation because I was feeling some kind of way.

One-View was broken herself. I was even wrong bringing this issue to her. The selfishness had risen again. It was all about me. My emotions were getting the best of me. One-View had just experienced a major catastrophe in her life that occurred a week or two prior to the Listener's mom passing away. Was this normal for me? Am I one of those messy, drama queens you hear about? No! No, I am not! This was not normal for me. I usually keep people, including family, out of my personal business when it comes to relationships. I have learned from others that when you involve people, especially family in your business, they form an opinion on your mate based on something that happened to you, or was said to you by the mate. Perhaps, you and your mate can have a disagreement, and maybe the conversation escalates to yelling, or saying things you don't really mean.

You and your mate make up apologize, but because you involved your family or friends, being that they love you and want what is best for you, they cannot get over the issue that had nothing to do with them. They are at odds with your mate and you find yourself trying to make amends between your mate and them. My timing was horrible and off on so many levels. I should have been talking to God, but no, all of a sudden, I felt the need to talk to someone.

I wish that I had an understanding of Galatians 5:16,17 at the time. I needed sound doctrine to help me through. I needed to have been walking by the spirit. In that present state, I would have spoken to a stranger if I could have. One-View and I started talking, again about a conversation I should have not been having with her. It should have been me being supportive of her and making sure her state-of-mind was good. I explained the situation to One-View, and she proceeded to ask me when was the last time I seen the Listener.

I told her the last time I had seen the Listener was for my birthday dinner. The Listener took me out to dinner for my birthday.

One-View said, "Oh, no, Kim, that is not good."

Out of the blue, One-View asked me permission to look on the Listener's social media page. My response was sure, no problem. Well, it was a problem because I was operating out of my flesh, number one, and secondly, I should have kept One-View out of the situation. Thirdly, when you go playing Sherlock Holmes, you have to be prepared for what you may discover; it may be more than what you bargained for. The discovery may be hazardous to your health or state-of-mind. Lastly, two broken people is a recipe for disaster. While we were on the phone, One-View went to the Listener's social media page. One-View asked me to go and look on another woman's social page that I did not know. Allow me rewind a little, bit here.

I knew that the Listener's page was full of positive quotes, scriptures, nothing bad, so for me to tell her it was okay to go on his page was not a problem in my mind. In my spirit, though, it did not feel right. I was hesitant when I said yes. A small voice kept saying, *No, don't do it. No, Kim, don't do it.*

One-view said, "Please, just go on the page and look."

My flesh said, "Okay, I will." I looked and saw the Listener on that page with that woman together. I was so sorrowful. I was in shock and

I could not believe my eyes. My flesh went there. I asked myself, "Why? Why now?"

Why would he do something like this? This does not make any sense at all. This is not the character of the man that I knew. If he is involved with this lady, why would he disrespect her and take me out to dinner?"

We are not having sex, so he is definitely not here for the sex. What is this? He does not owe me anything. He is not being financially supported by me. He has been a straight forward man with me. Does he feel sorry for me? But he has been helping me, so I am confused. What about the other woman? That is not fair to her. She does not know that I exist. WHAT IS THIS! The carnality thinking was running loose and on a rampage in my mind.

In anger, I decided to call the Listener. My flesh was saying you give him a piece of your mind. When he answered the phone, I could not go off on him. Why is that? I was feeling angry; he needed to hear a piece of my mind. It was like something else was happening. I could not talk crazy at all. Why, why, why!-

The conversation went as follows:

"Hello," the Listener answered.

"Are you at work or at home?" I asked, "I would like say some things to you."

"I am just about at work, but I have some time to listen," he said.

"Well, I prefer when you have time to talk, that you call me because I really need to say some things to you," My tone was pleasant, it was my normal self. How is this happening? I wanted to be sarcastic, cold and callous, but that was not going to work.

"Go ahead and talk," the Listener said.

Did I cut to the chase? or go around about to say what I wanted to say? Yes, around about is what I did.

"In life, I have come to understand that, you love who you love. Just because you love someone, does not mean that they love you," I paused.

The Listener remained quiet not interrupting.

"I love you with all of my heart and I see that you chose someone," I paused.

The Listener remained quiet not interrupting.

"I want to thank you for everything you have done for me, for helping me. I will always love you for that."

Confused the Listener said, "What are you talking about?"

I got extremely quite.

"I chose someone? I do not know what you are talking about," it was apparent that the Listener did not have a clue what I was talking about.

"There are a lot of women that like me, who want to be with me," he said.

I interrupted before he could finish his sentence, "Yes, I know, that is true. I told you that when we first met. You said, No. I said, Yes."

"You are the man. The Bible says that a man that finds a wife finds a good thing.

The Listener remained quiet, so I continued, "It does not matter how many women like you or want to be with you. It is who you choose to be with."

Still the Listener said nothing.

"You have the choice to choose," I said.

"Look, I have just lost my mother, I have to bury my mother, and deal with that," He said sternly and calmly.

I got quiet.

"I really do not have the time to worry about what you think," he said.

Once again, Interrupting, not letting him finish, I said, "I know you lost your mother, I have called you, texted you, and social media message you. Trying to reach out and be supportive."

There was silence before he replied, "I know, I got all of your messages and I thanked you for the support."

I did not respond.

"I only have two uncles left, I need to visit them. I am trying to figure out what I am going to do," he said in a hurt voice. I can tell this was him crying out.

I got quiet.

The Listener then became angry and replied, "It is just me and my siblings, so right now, I really do not care what you think."

Feeling of shock and hurt overtook me.

"You do not think that I would be man enough to tell you the truth. Haven't I been truthful to you?" he asked.

"Yes, you have been" I added.

The Listener responded over me, "If you think I would do something like that and not communicate with you, then maybe you really don't know me."

Again, I was quiet.

"You need to focus on God and let Him work everything out," he said.

I remained silent and in shock.

"Okay, well, you have a good day at work, I hope you will call from time to time, we're friends first," I said trying to shake the shock.

"I will," he assured me.

After I got off of that phone from that conversation, I called Oneview again to talk about what happened. I had not learned the lesson. I was sinking further. This entire fiasco hit me like a locomotive. I cried. I screamed so loud that I am sure, I was heard a block away. Jesus! Jesus! Jesus! Help me, Jesus! Help me! I screamed and cried. I could not breathe for the first time in a relationship situation. This relationship was not me helping somebody else. It was not running into a relationship to get away from someone else, nor a substitute partial husband. This was about me. Jesus had to help me catch my breath. I did not eat or sleep for three days. Believe me, I tried to eat and sleep.

I would get in the bed at night and cry Jesus! Jesus! Help me! Jesus! I trust you Jesus! I trust you Jesus! I was just sobbing. It was now Sunday and I had to fight to get myself together to go to church. My flesh was agreeing with what the enemy was saying. No, stay home, you are hurt, you do not want to be around other people right now. If you start talking to others, it is only going to make things worse. You will surely not feel better or get better, so what is the use?

Chapter 32

Sister Soldier Took Me to Church

Another relative called me and I will refer to her as Sister Soldier. Sister Soldier said, "You up for church? You getting ready? I overslept. "Yes. I am up" I replied.

Before I could give an excuse, she said, "I will be out front at 9:15 or 9:20am"
"Okay?"I said.
We hung up.
When the daughter that lives with me had to work on Sundays, Sister Soldier came to pick me up. this was one of those Sundays. I got myself ready and at 9:15am sharp she was there. When I got in the car I was quiet, but the tears were rolling down my face. Sister Soldier did not ask me what was wrong, She knew the circumstances that caused the tears, and she did not say one word.

When we got to the church, parking, for some reason, looked scarce and since I walk with a cane, Sister Soldier said, "You go in find the seats and I will park. I will be right in."

We are normally early to find our seats, greet other saints, get comfortable, and be there for opening prayer. This day we were behind schedule, but God is good. The Father had a word for me and I believe in my heart that the devil did not want me to get that life changing Word. I did not know that the word was not going to come through my spiritual father, but come through one of his spiritual sons. Thank you, Father, for taking care of your daughter.

I walked in the church, trying to hold myself together and before I could try to find a seat the elder said, "Grab your neighbors hand and let's pray." Everyone stopped where they were and grabbed the hand of the person next to them. There was a lady right where I was standing, so I grabbed her hand.

All I know is…from the moment I grabbed the lady's hand, bowed my head, and closed my eyes, I began to cry. I was sobbing uncontrollably. When the prayer was over, the lady dropped my hand, turned to her left and began to talk to the people she knew that were on her left. I walked towards a seat and looked for a box of tissue that sat in one of the baskets at the end of some of the church rows. I got some tissue and continued to walk to find myself a seat. By the time I found the seat, Sister Soldier was right behind me. We sat down. The praise and worship team started praise and worship.

I stood up with trouble. I was struggling, but I was going to do all I could to praise God. Talk about faith to praise, even when you do not feel like it. I stood up and put my hands up over my head with all my might. While the tears were streaming down my face, my heart was so heavy. I could only raise my hands and cry. I tried to sing, but it was not working. Even so, my hands were raised. During the beginning of praise and worship, I cried and by the time it was over I was sitting, no strength to stand, with my head down, eyes full of tears, sobbing. The usher passed me a box of tissue. I was a broken mess.

On top of this, the elder said, "Say hello to your neighbor. The person sitting next to you, in front of you and behind you."

I was saying, in my head, "Really, Really?" I did not want to say hello to anyone.

The Elder said, "Tell them your name and say, 'It is good to see you in the House of the Lord.'"

I turned to my left side and there was a tall young and handsome brother sitting there next to me. *Why? Why? Why?*

I turned and looked at this man, who I did not want to turn and look at, and apologized. I said, "I am so sorry you had to be sitting next to someone crying."

He said, "Aw, it's alright." He pat me on the back".

We even had a guest pastor preaching because our pastor was out of town. The guest pastor got in the pulpit and started to pray. The handsome brother on the left put his hand on my hand. I was still crying and he prayed for me. I needed all the prayer I could get. Then, after he prayed, this pastor announced the subject he was preaching on. You will never guess what the message was. Never mind. I will not keep you in suspense. It was "WHY."

Can you believe it? I am asking God why, and he is about to preach why. I was done. Take me out of the oven, I was done. I'm saying, "Oh, my God!" What a message to be preaching at this time. I was not ready for this. It was a life changing message. It was an answered prayer message. I wish I could give everyone that wants to know why for the trials and tribulations of their lives, a copy of that message.

I did not get the explanation as to the why in my life at that moment, but what was happening for me was a supernatural surgery and I did not know it. My faith was going to increase, and my relationship with the Father was about to become closer than it ever had been. I was about to know how to trust God, in the storm, during the storm, and as I was to come out of the storm. My, my, my. A new thing was happening in me.

When the pastor went to the word of God and quoted the scripture from James Chapter One, verses two through four, which says in the King James Version of the Bible; "My brethren, count it all joy when ye fall into divers temptations. Knowing this, that the trying of your faith worketh patience. But let patience have her perfect work, that ye may be perfect and entire, wanting nothing."

At the end of the sermon, he did an altar call, and I went to the altar for prayer. This counting it all joy, was something that I was not getting. I was not feeling joyous. I was feeling hurt. I cried all the way to the altar. I was crying a river. Just call me the crying sister. As I got close to the altar, one of the altar workers asked me if I needed a chair because I walked with a cane. I said, "No, thank you."

The guest pastor prayed for all of those who were at the altar, including me. I cried in the arms of an altar worker during the prayer. I told you, I was the crying sister. After the prayer, all those at the altar were taken to a room where the altar workers have additional prayer. They gave information needed for the individual, whether it was leading someone to Christ, preparing a baptismal candidate, counseling in a certain area, and much more.

Chapter 33

Leaving The Altar And Here Comes The Eloquent Warrior!

Once I sat down in the room, the altar worker talked to me, but there was another person who was sitting beside the altar worker. My head was down, and I was still crying. The other person grabbed my face, raised my head up and said, "Look at me." I looked, and it was someone I recognized, someone I knew personally. I grabbed her and I hugged her so tight and cried. I will refer to her as Eloquent Warrior. The younger relative was now talking to the oldest relative, as if the roles were reversed.

Eloquent Warrior said, "So this is what we do now? Why didn't you call me? Why are we here? You know you could have called me. You got us up in here? We could have taken care of this at home, not up in here."

The altar worker said, "You know her?"

Eloquent Warrior said, "Yes, this is my relative."

The Eloquent Warrior was awaiting an answer.

I tried to get my composure together, "When it comes to my personal life, I am so used to handling my own business and leaving everyone else out," I replied.

I told Eloquent Warrior that I knew she had a full plate that was overflowing, and I did not feel she needed to deal with my situations. I thought about calling, but I did not call. I was not going to burden Eloquent Warrior with my issues.

"But we could have fixed this at home, not here. We are family. You help me. I call on you when I need you; so, you don't think I would do the same thing for you?" she asked.

"I know you would have,: I said, but I am the oldest and I feel like I should be setting the example."

It was time to go, the altar worker, Eloquent Warrior, and I had prayer before we left. The Eloquent Warrior said, "Come by the house and we can talk about it at home."

"Okay," I said.

Let me clarify something before I go any further. The Eloquent Warrior was not saying that you cannot get the proper help at church. She was saying we are women of faith and have a relationship with God. We could have solved the issue, prayed about the issue among ourselves, and if after doing all we know to do and needed the church involved, then we go to the church.

> *Older women likewise are to be reverent in their behavior, not malicious gossips nor enslaved to much wine, teaching what is good, so that they may encourage the young women to love their husbands, to love their children, to be sensible, pure, workers at home, kind, being subject to their own husbands, so that the word of God will not be dishonored.*
> —Titus 2:3-5(NAS)

The Eloquent Warrior had no idea I was hurting and it bothered her. She loves me, this I know. We have been through alot and have gotten through trials and tribulations talking to each other and praying for one another, so what changed, was what she really wanted to understand. How could I just go from 0 to two hundred? How could I go to the extreme? Why was this situation so different from any of the other talks that we had? Why did I try to stay isolated from others, but especially her? I did not have an answer for her.

Anyway, I felt a little better. I was given information to contact the counselor's office for counseling and prayer to help with what I was dealing with, which we never talked about what it was that was going on with me. Crazy! I guess it was taking too long for the altar worker to help me, and I guess whoever wanted her to hurry along was ready to close up shop per se. She was not trying to rush, but they wanted her to give me information so I could call the counseling services and get further assistance. Everything happens for a reason and I am sure that was going to be revealed in time. I never went by the Eloquent Warrior's house after church. I just could not bring myself to do it. I felt so weighted down.

Chapter 34

Sister Soldier And I At The Beach

Remember Sister Soldier brought me to church and was taking me back home. When Sister Soldier and I were on our way back to my house, I asked would she like to go to the beach. She said, sure. When we got in my house, the spirit said, "Get a pair of shorts and some sandals for Sister Soldier."

I asked Sister Soldier if she wanted to just wear a pair of shorts and sandals and we go to the beach from here. She said sure and that's what we did. I needed to go to the beach to clear my head and pray. Sister Soldier and I stayed at the beach the rest of the afternoon. It was hot and beautiful, but most importantly, peaceful.

While at the beach, I prayed to God about my situation. I prayed for friends and family. When I prayed about the situation, I asked God to forgive me for not doing what He asked me to do. The Lord had asked me a year ago, to focus on Him and that he would take care of everything else around me. Here I was, a year later, and I had allowed my flesh to rise up and be disobedient. I felt so bad. I prayed for the Listener, his family and for myself. There was a moment while I was standing in the water, the Lord spoke to my spirit.

The Lord said, "Do you see the waves?"

"Yes, Lord, I see the waves."

"I want you to look out as far as you can see; you see all of those waves?" He asked.

"Yes, Lord, I see them."

"I want you to look at those waves."

"Okay." I did what He asked.

The Lord then said, "Do you see that some of the waves are small, some are medium, some are large, and some you can barely see?"

"Yes, Lord, I see that."

Next, he said, "All those waves you are looking at are trials and tribulations."

He said, "Sometimes they will come small, medium, and large. They will come Large, small, large, even larger, sometimes a massive wave. Then it will smooth out for a bit."

I was out in the waves, talking to the Lord and all the people that were out there did not bother me. I was standing in the water while the Lord was talking to me and the waves were coming at me. Some of the waves were knocking me around. I told the Lord I was listening because I was really getting knocked around a little, but not too much, just enough to get and keep my attention.

The Lord said, "Do you know what your job is to do while the trials and tribulations come?" I really did not get the chance to respond. He said, "Your job is to stand. Stand on my Word." The waves were getting more intense as they were hitting me, but I stood there and listened. The Lord said, "When the trials and tribulations come, they may knock you around, but stand on my Word. They may knock you down, get back up and stand on my Word. Some will come and smooth out. Some may be massive, but you still stand on my Word".

"Thank you, Lord!" I cried out. I began to worship and praise the Lord. I could care less if anyone was watching me or hearing me out at the beach. I needed the Father and the Father was giving me revelation right where I was. It is good to know that the Father does not have to wait until you are in a church to communicate with you. The Father can speak to you in your house, your car, walking down the street, a job, or like with me at the beach. When the Father speaks, I just want to be able to hear him wheresoever I am, listen to what He says and because I listened, I should be applying what He has said to my life.

I yelled for Sister Soldier to come to the water because at the time she was lying down on the blanket. When she came over to the water, I told her what the Lord, had said.

We prayed and praised the Lord and had a wonderful time in the Lord at the beach. It was getting late, so we decided it was time to go home. It was good that it was late in my mind because I knew all I had to do was go home, take a shower, and get in the bed. No idle time for the mind to think, just go to sleep.

I got home, took my shower, got in the bed and it seemed as though somebody came in my head and said, "No silence in this mind. She needs to think about how she felt before the beach." I was having trouble.

I was saying to myself, *Oh! No! Help me, Lord. My life is in a crisis.*

All I could do was lay in my bed and say, "Jesus! Jesus! Jesus! Help me, Jesus! I trust you, Jesus! You are all I have, Jesus!" I continued saying this until I was sleep.

Chapter 35

I Was Making Things Worse

The next morning, I called, Eloquent Warrior.

When she answered, I said, "Eloquent Warrior, please, please, pray for me. I am having trouble this morning. I am really struggling and I tossed and turned all night."

"Why don't you come by and we can talk," she insisted.

I said, "Well, One-View and her fiancé are supposed to be picking me up and taking me to the beach today. So I am going to go back today and try to clear my head. Just pray for me."

Eloquent Warrior said, "I always do that."

"Okay." I got off the phone.

It was getting late and I did not think I was going to be able to go to the beach. One-View and her fiancé called they were running a little late because they had some errands to take care of, but they were coming. They finally arrived and they took me to a different beach than where Sister Soldier and I went to. We sat, watched the waves, they were trying to help me, they wanted an explanation of what was going on about the pictures and why the Listener was being so distant from me. It was out of their love for me and knowing how I felt about the Listener. I cried because I was back to the same attitude I had before the social media.

Again, I wanted to get angry and go off, but I could not. I could only say good things about our relationship and his treatment of me since I had known him. I made a dumb decision earlier that morning before I went to the beach, which is out of my character. I decided to go on social media, screenshot a couple of pictures and send it to him in a text message. I guess you call that putting him on blast. I wanted to send the information that I had seen and texted it to him. I wanted an explanation.

I had no reason to be or feel jealous since I met him and now because of this photo with a woman, jealousy rises. Trust was never an issue, so why now. I am confused about what's really going on with me.

It was late and the Listener, must have just gotten off of work, saw the text and responded. The response was not what I had anticipated.

He responded, "Nice pictures. In a relationship, I'm shocked. You have gone on someone else's page, and put it in a text to me. You have come to a conclusion in your head and I understand."

I texted back, "No, I do not want to come to a conclusion, I want an explanation. I want to see you face-to-face."

"No," he said.

"If I ever meant anything to you, you would meet me," I said.

No response.

The lack of response just super-sized my pain and frustrations. I was just trying to fix things and I was completely messing things up. Disobedient! Disobedient! Disobedient! The Lord said to FOCUS! Focus on Him and He would take care of everything else around me. Obedience is better than sacrifice. One-View and her fiancé took me home, and when I got home, I did not want to sit or think.

Chapter 36

The Elegant Warrior Said, "Shut Up! Consider The Source!"

I called Eloquent Warrior. If you remember, the Eloquent Warrior had been trying to get me to her house to talk since church on Sunday, and it probably seemed as though, I was giving her excuses, and now I have no other choice because I really need her.

I asked Eloquent Warrior if I could come by the house to talk and she said, "Yes."

I asked my daughter if I could drive her car to Eloquent Warrior's house for a little bit. I did not want to be at home because I could not keep from crying and I did not want my daughter asking me questions, even though I knew she knew something was wrong with her mother, but it was not her business. I have always been annoyed with adults that bring their children in their personal business as if they are equal. Let the child be the child and the adult be the adult. You experiences as an adult should be able to help your child. The child has not even experienced life. They cannot help you with your problems and have not experienced life themselves. When I got to Eloquent Warrior's house we sat down and I told her everything that happened.

She listened to everything and when I was done speaking she said, "Wait a minute, didn't you say this man just lost his mother?"

I said, "Yes."

Eloquent Warrior said, "I need you to Shut up!"

"What?" I said.

"I said Shut up! You are not allowing this man to grieve his mother. You're coming to this man with this foolishness! How did you get this information anyway?"she asked.

I told her that One-View came across the information and made me aware of it. Eloquent Warrior said, "And how did she find this information?"

Not really sure, I said, "I do not know. She lucked up on it, when she went on his social media page."

"Question, did you consider the source?" she asked.

"No, I did not consider the source." after thinking about it I replied.

"Well I need you to be quiet now," she insisted.

I got ready to say something. She said, "No! I really need you to be quiet, because I do not hear this relationship is over in the Spirit. Allow this man to grieve his mother," Eloquent Warrior insisted.

Giving up, I said, "Okay."

We talked about some other things and I left for the night home. I was grateful that Eloquent Warrior knows me well enough, to see I needed help, and she has a relationship with God, where she was sensitive to the Spirit of God, to hear what God was saying. I meditated on the conversation I had with Eloquent Warrior. I prayed to the Lord on the way to the house.

"Lord, I am sorry, let the Listener know my intentions were not to be inconsiderate. I did not mean him any harm." I got home, took a shower and got in the bed. It had become a recipe to try to get some sleep by calling on the Lord. "Jesus! Jesus! Help me! Jesus! Jesus! I trust you! I trust you! Jesus! Jesus! Jesus!"

I prefer to call on the name of the Lord, than to indulge in alcoholic beverages, or some other substance that would only dull my senses, then when I wake up I am still faced with the same issues I was dealing with before I went to sleep. Calling on the name of the Lord was helping me keep my mind stayed on him and the perfect peace helped me sleep.

Chapter 37

Tell Your Story

The next morning, I got up and called Eloquent Warrior. When she answered the phone, she said, "I texted you. Did you get my text?"

I said, "No, what did it say?"

"I just texted you to see if you wanted to get out of the house,"

"YES! Yes, I do. That is why I was calling you," I said, wanting to get out of the house more than anything.

"Okay, give me thirty minutes and I will be there," she said.

When Eloquent Warrior arrived, she was with her youngest daughter, two lady friends, and one had her daughter. One of the lady friends, the one that did not have a daughter in the truck, was going to be dropped off at the Amtrak Station. The plan was that they were going to do a few errands, then take the lady friend leaving town to the train station. Once the lady was dropped off at the train station, the other lady, the kids, Eloquent Warrior went to Eloquent Warrior's house. We arrived at the house, Eloquent Warrior told the kids to go and play. She then asked me if I was hungry because she had some food left over from the party at her house the night before.

I replied, "Yes, but only a little, I have not eaten in three days."

Eloquent Warrior said, "Yes, you need to eat something, that's not good. The friend with the daughter, Eloquent Warrior and I ate.

"How are you doing?" she asked because I was quiet the entire time. I really was not much for conversation.

My response was, "I'm hurting, but okay."

The friend had no clue what was going on, but she could tell that I was hurting, I'm sure of that.

I decided to talk about it, which invited the friend in the conversation. The friend comforted me with a hug. Suddenly, I felt an overwhelming need to speak of all the positive and wonderful things that had come to my mind about the Listener. The friend said, I wish I had that. Eloquent Warrior told the friend to tell me what happened to her.

When the friend began to explain what happened in the relationship she was involved in something began to happen to me. I had to get up because it was as if an invisible vacuum cleaner was suctioning up all my hurts that I was going through, all the emotions that I had been feeling. Everything that I had been through since the onset of this situation was being sucked up in an invisible vacuum cleaner. It spiritually was being vacuumed up. The pain was all gone. It seemed as though it was vacuumed up and placed in my back pocket of my jeans, sort of speak.

I knew from that moment, I was different, changed. I stopped the conversation for a minute. I chuckled and said, "God you are something else," I chuckled again. "You have gotten my attention." I raised my hands above my head and said, "Father, I thank you and I praise you!"

Immediately after that, I began to talk to the friend. The friend was dealing with some issues concerning a man that she was in a relationship with. Her relationship was on and off with this man. Sometimes we are warned about people ahead of time and do not listen. Then there are situations where an individual will tell you up front, what the person wants out of the relationship, but some of us females feel that once we get involved with the guy, we can change his thinking, we can change the weaknesses in his life and make him stronger and everything would be perfect or going to be okay. This was one of those situations for this young lady and here I was now helping her and comforting her.

Wow, I said, "Father, I see, I see what you are doing here." I was ready to go home now.

The Eloquent Warrior dropped me off at home. When I got in my house, I had a new pep in my step. I started talking to the Lord. "Lord, you are something else, you got my attention, and I get it now. You told me to focus on you and you would take care of everything around me, but I had my focus mostly on the Listener."

Talking to God, I said, "I was in my own selfish way, messing things up. I was not trusting you completely. I was trusting in my own ability. Forgive me, Lord!"

As you are reading my story, I do not want you to think that I am no longer in self. I do not want you to think that I do not mess up anymore. I have to die daily of self to become more like Christ. Even though I am in the flesh, but born again of the water and the spirit, it does not give me an excuse to live my life like the world, knowing I am not of it. God reminds me often to focus on Him like He told me to. Often I find myself still walking in the life of I. Kim, what do you mean by the life of I? I can't do, I am not, and I do not want to; this is what I mean by the life of I. God told me to do, which was a command. He did not ask me if wanted to do, or can I do.

Therefore, we do not lose heart, but though our outer man is decaying, yet our inner man is being renewed day by day. 2Corinthians 4:16(NAS)

THE LORD SAID:

The Lord said, "It is time to go to school and it is time to write a book," which is this book I am writing now. I started school on August 31, 2015. I started writing this book three days later. I was chasing after one man to be in my life as a Dad. God placed another man in my life to help me see that my help, my answers, truly come from the Lord. Everything I needed in my life was in **The Father**. I had to remember that Jesus and the Father are ONE.

> *I will lift up mine eyes unto the hills, from whence cometh my help. My help cometh from the Lord, which made heaven and earth.*
>
> —Psalms 121:1,2(KJV)

She will give birth to a son, and you are to give him the name Jesus, because he will save his people from their sins." All this took place to fulfill what the Lord had said through the prophet. The virgin will conceive and give birth to a son, and they will call him Immanuel" (which means "God with us").

—**Matthew 1:21-23, (NIV)**

For a child has been born- for us! The gift of a son-for us! He'll take over the running of the world. His names will be Amazing Counselor, Strong God.. Eternal Father, Prince of Wholeness. His ruling authority will grow, and there'll be no limit to the wholeness he brings. He'll rule from the historic David throne over that promised kingdom. He'll put that kingdom on a firm footing and keep it going with fair dealing and right living, beginning now and lasting always. The zeal of God-of-the-Angel-armies will do all this.

—**Isaiah 9:6, 7, (MSG)**

Chapter 38

How Are You And The Listener?

Wondering what's happening now in the Listener and my life? I revisited the social media page. I looked at the pictures and I felt like a fool. I was in the right frame of mind to look at the picks this time. I noticed that the picks were old; he looked different from the way he presently looks. Why was I not able to see that the first time? I apologized to the Listener, first, for not allowing him to grieve for his mother. I also apologized for the way I went about things. I told him that I would be here praying that God heals and comforts his heart in his time of grieving for the loss of his mother. I explained to the Listener that I was apologizing for my behavior because if I had lost one of my parents, I would have not been entertaining anyone's foolishness either.

I do not know what it is like to lose a mother, a father; I still have my ninety-four-year old grandmother living. One day they will go home to glory, to be with the Father and I, too, will need friends and family praying for me. One thing is for sure; I made the best of everyday when it came to this relationship that we had together and I did not, nor do I, have any regrets. It has been an amazing learning experience. I love living in the land of no regrets. Why do something you are going to regret? In the land of no regrets, I hold on to the positive things, and all the good times I had. Too many people hold on to every negative event, after a relationship has come to an end, whether both individuals decide to move on with their lives, they do not get along anymore, or even the way they see or think is different; leading them on different paths. The negative cannot be what defines the relationship that you had with the person that you once thought the world of.

Tomorrow is not promised so we must make the best of our relationships today. What relationship we have now, at this present moment. You can complain yourself into misery, only to lose the relationship, start over again and realize, what you had was not so bad after all. What we call trash, when it is not, will be someone else's treasure. The new person will make the best of the new relationship, begin to motivate, elevate, and appreciate the person to the point they will bring out their true treasure. You, on the outside, will feel as though they have done better in the new relationship than with you.

Always weigh your options and write down all the good and bad attributes of the person you are in a relationship with and if the good outways the bad. Well, you know what to do. Is the problem the other person? Or is the problem really you?

The Listener and I are both growing in the Lord. We both are getting better and better, each and every day, in each and every way.

We are being transformed by God into the man and woman He has designed for us to become. For God does know the plans that he has for the two of us for our future. We are both just trusting God to work everything out for our good. We both continue to lift each other in prayer. Life is better because I am finally focused on God and allowing Him to take care of everything around me. The most important thing is that I have learned from my past.

I am ten times better at listening, and I am moving forward and not backwards. This does not mean that I will not make any more mistakes in life because I will. This, by far, is no easy task, but with God, all things are possible. When I start to feel overwhelmed, I have to ask myself, "Am I trying to fix it, or am I going to leave it in God's hands? I know that as long as I live in this body, my spirit and my flesh will be at war, so it is up to me to daily work towards being an imitator of Christ. Do you know what the future holds for you and the Listener? No, I do not know, but the Father does. He knows everything.

LISTENING IS IMPORTANT

As this story comes to an end I must say, this journey, I am truly grateful for. I am thankful for my heavenly Father because in everything the Father does, He does it well. God above all gets all the honor and glory. I was a vessel used to remind my dad of who the Father is to him. The Father sent a vessel to me to remind me of who He is to me. When I wanted to do things my way, I began to botch things up. The Father reminded me that I need Him in order to live in this life. I had to learn the skill set of listening. Listening is a skill set one must learn how to do. The skill of listening is a skill many people lack. Most people are selective listeners, they only listen to what they want to hear; that which sounds good to them. There is a time and a place to be in control of my life.

I can't allow others to control my life. The life I live is because of my choices and no one else's; so it is imperative that I make the proper choices for my life. My destiny is in my hands and mouth. It is not always how you start, or how many times you had to start over, it is how you are going to end up because of that choice. Your start may have been rough, tragic, undesirable, destructive, or disastrous, but with God, your life can change for the good. "For to live is Christ."

Nothing in your life will be in vain because you will be in the position to help someone else. I began to make the vessel that was there to help me the center of my attention, an idol. The Lord said in His Word that he would not have any other gods before Him. The Father sent an earthquake to get my attention off of the vessel for a lack of listening on my part, to look to the Father and not to man for answers. The Father also showed me that I must consider the source of information that I receive from anyone, pray and get the facts before reacting under false pretenses.

There are two walks to choose from, two different paths to take, two ways to think. You can choose to walk with Christ or the devil. You can take God's way of doing things path, or you can take the world's way of doing things, which is led by the flesh and your selfish pride. You can think of how you would do things or how God would do things. I am not saying that this is easy to do because it is not. This is a process and, as long as I live on earth, there is an adversary going to and fro seeking whom he may destroy by using our weakness against us. In all my getting, I must get an understanding. I need to count the cost, think, ponder, before I make moves. as the Bible says.

Chapter 39

How Is Your Relationship With The Father And Your Dad?

My dad is my dad, and I love him. He is doing well and living his life for the Lord. This book was not about him, but because it started with him, I thought I would share. Today, I have a great relationship with my dad. Now, my dad and I have a normal father-daughter relationship. Where I was looking for my dad before, things have changed. I am looking for and to the Father, from which comes my help. I am letting you know because you cannot go backwards, but you can heal from the past and start a new relationship with your parent, right where you are.

It is my job to focus on the Father and believe Him that everything will be taken care of around me. The Father said that those who seek Him will find Him. The Father told me to knock and the door shall be opened unto me. I feel like the door is wide open. The Father's love for me is unconditional. I feel like I have been given a fresh start in life with the Father directing my steps. I have found me. I know what I want and can think for myself. I matter.

In conclusion, The Father is now a love song that plays and stays on my mind and in my heart. When I think about the Father, it puts a smile on my face because of his love for me. Learning more about the Father made me fall in love with Him. I know that the Father loves me just the way I am, and I do not have to live up to the standards of man. Man is always capable of disappointing you, but the Father never will. He is the same today, yesterday, and will be tomorrow.

Happiness is not found in man, but it is found in right relationship with the Father. The Father knew that if I learned about his love for me, it would give me the desire to please him. It would make me change to be the best me I could possibly be with His help. Remember when I said that the Listener was the first man that saw me. The Listener saw right through me. He understood me and was the first man that directed me back to the Father. Well, I was wrong. The Father saw me and knew me first. The Father saw me and sent the Listener to help me find my way back to Him.

I learned that the Father uses others to pray with you through your trials and tribulations. We are never alone, unless we choose to be. I have learned it is up to me to make the right choices. Your present situations you are in are the results of the choices you made. The good thing is that because we have the freedom of choice, if we do not like our present situation, we can choose to change it. I learned that people come into our lives for a reason. All relationships are not for a lifetime, but for seasons. I learned that all unpleasant circumstances are not always the devil. We, as individuals, put ourselves in unpleasant circumstances at times, and some things God just allows to happen, and we do not have the "why" explanation. God designed it all in a way that He alone would get the glory, not man. Again, we did not create God, God created us in His image.

Things that happen to us sometimes are to increase our faith in my opinion as well. We should desire to see God's glory manifested in our lives. I thank God that the past is behind me, and I am moving forward. I am living the best, blessed days of my life now! Forever changing for the better and growing more and more in Christ. The only reason I am living my best, blessed days now is because I have decided to leave the old me behind—the sin ful Kim—and move forward in Christ. I am focused on the Father, which is the way, the truth, and the life. It is a lot of work, very challenging at times, but it is apart of the race. I have to run the race, and keep my eyes on the prize.

Closing Prayer

"Now, Father, I know that you are the Father of all creation. I was looking for my dad, and I should have been looking to you, Father. Father, I pray that everyone that took the time to read this book, that you bless them. Father, I pray that you have made a difference in their lives for the better. I pray that you give them the ability, along with the faith, to trust you implicitly, in every area of their lives. Father, in the gift of choice you gave us, help them to be wise in their choices that they make. Let each man and woman examine themselves to see if the choices that they are making are choices you would agree with. Time is precious, valuable, and just about up. We will have to answer for the things we have done in this life.

Father, you know that we can never be perfect, but we are without excuses because we have you to look to. Help us, Father, to surrender our lives to you. Help each and every one of the readers of this book see that you thought we were worth saving Father. Father, living our lives for you is progressive, because every day we wake up to you, we must die daily to sin, which is not an easy task. Father, help us to understand that you are here with us, and the physical representation that we have of you is your Word. Father, we live in a sinful world, full of distractions and you have given us a way of escape. Father, I rebuke and bind every demonic spirit or force of ungodly distractions, ungodly living, in the lives of the reader of this book. Father, rest in the readers' lives, rest in their mind and hearts. I decree and declare a fresh anointing of God-given strength, God-given endurance, God-given faith, and God-given wisdom to walk in the victorious life you have designed for them, all in Jesus Name!

My brother, my sister, thank you for reading the book. Our God is an amazing God, and He really is full of grace, mercy and truth. May God's grace and mercy be extended to you in Jesus Name, To God Be The Glory, forever more, Amen!

His Help

When I say "His" help, I am not saying that I helped myself. I am saying that with His help, the Father, gave me help to propel my life forward in Him. The help came through certain books I was led to read, or through people He sent my way. I could not get better without His help. There were times when I would just sit in my room, pray and ask God what is it that I needed to do. I wrote in journals. I fasted, if I was led to fast. I would play praise and worship music or gospel music. I would meditate on God's word. My favorite place to go was to the beach, to meditate or to just sit and watch the waves.

When I was little, my mother would take my brother and me to the beach and we'd stand in the water. As the waves would come toward us, she would say, "All the positive things come in," and as the waves would go out, she would say, "All the negative things go out." I would write in the sand and pray to God about the things I wanted and needed. As the waves would come in and wash it away, I would thank God, as if he received what I said and, in due season, it would come to pass.

When you are going through a healing process there are several levels to break through, depending on the individual. My healing needed to start from my childhood. During this healing process, it was important for me to be around positive people when I was around people. I would not just stay cooped up in the house, isolated from everything and everyone all the time. That was not healthy. There were times that I needed to be alone with me so I could learn who I was. Learning how to live with yourself, do things by yourself, encourage yourself, and love yourself, this is work. I had to start working out, which was part of working on me, the temple that the Holy Spirit dwells in. At first, I wanted to initially get in shape to get my figure back-my sexy back, as some call it. The exercising helped me to think clearer, meditate, and focus. After dealing with so much suffering from my work injury and finding out that the weight would make my physical health worse. It turned into a situation of, "Let me get this weight off of me so my knees and back do not hurt so bad." It was a health issue.

I needed to take care of the temple so that it was physically healthy and strong. It needed to be spiritually and physically healthy and strong. It is a losing battle, every time you go out into the world with no spiritual guidance, an unequipped soldier, not knowing what the word of God says for one of the weapons being used on you in the world. An equipped soldier is sound in doctrine. The more doctrine he or she learns, the more skilled you become as a soldier. Along the way, the commander and chief, God, will send other soldiers out with you or to you that can help you fight the war. The Father is so awesome because when He goes to work on you, He works on several areas, at the same time, so that when it is time to go to war, you are ready for the battle. He does not stop working on you. He is continuously working on us to become that supreme soldier, that supernatural soldier, the soldier that He will say, "Well Done!"

Words I Meditate On

Put aside those attitudes that do not fit who we are and what you do not want in your life.

Focus on the needs of others. Ask God to help you develop the character of kindness. Practice being kind, which is a quality of Almighty God.

If you can kill it in your head, you can kill it in your life.

I need to be the highest and best version of myself.

Anything I am trying to transform is a process. Every transformation takes time, and I cannot let people make me give up on the process.

Each and every day, each and every way, I'm getting better and better.

I can do all things through Christ that strengthens me.

Be still and know that I am God.

The just shall live by faith.

No weapon formed against me shall prosper.

Your faith makes you whole.

Lord, conquer me to bless me.

Remain at peace, God will fight your battles.

I am a daughter of a King.

Books I Read

1. The Bible

2. *The 40 day Soul Fast (Your Journey to Authentic Living)* Author: Cindy Trimm

3. *Developing The Leader Within You* Author: John C. Maxwell

4. *Understanding The Purpose and Power of PRAYER Earthly License For Heavenly Interference* Author: Dr. Myles Munroe

5. *In His image (An intimate Reflection of God)* Author: Dr. Kenneth Ulmer

6. *Understanding the Purpose and Power of Woman* Author: Dr. Myles Munroe

7. *The Tongue: A Creative Force* Author: Charles Capps

8. *The People Factor* Author: Van Moody

9. *Commanding Your Morning* Author: Cindy Trimm

References

Bible Hub, New International Version
Bible Gateway, New International Version
New Living Translation Bible
King James Version
Message Bible
New American Standard Bible
www.thefreedictionary.com
www.natural healers.com
www.gty.org virgin birth by John MacArthur
www.patheos.com Joel J. Miller
seeds of the kingdom.org
Dr. Phil.com /Life Strategies/ Behave your way to success.
Oswald Chambers quote
www.oxforddictionaries.com
James Allen "As A Man Thinketh"
www.brainyquote.com
www.twistedsifter.com 10 Things You Don't Know About Chameleons
www.sevenreflections.

www.ingramcontent.com/pod-product-compliance
Lightning Source LLC
Chambersburg PA
CBHW031414290426
44110CB00011B/378